Comments on other *Amazing Stories* from readers & reviewers

"You might call them the non-fiction response to Harlequin romances: easy to consume and potentially addictive."
Robert Martin, *The Chronicle Herald*

"Tightly written volumes filled with lots of wit and humour about famous and infamous Canadians."
Eric Shackleton, *The Globe and Mail*

"This is popular history as it should be ... For this price, buy two and give one to a friend."
Terry Cook, a reader from Ottawa, on **Rebel Women**

"Stories are rich in description, and bristle with a clever, stylish realness."
Mark Weber, *Central Alberta Advisor,* on **Ghost Town Stories II**

"The resulting book is one readers will want to share with all the women in their lives."
Lynn Martel, *Rocky Mountain Outlook,* on **Women Explorers**

"[The books are] *long on plot and character and short on the sort of technical analysis that can be dreary for all but the most committed academic."*
Robert Martin, *The Chronicle Herald*

"A compelling read. Bertin ... has selected only the most intriguing tales, which she narrates with a wealth of detail."
Joyce Glasner, *New Brunswick Reader,* on **Strange Events**

"The heightened sense of drama and intrigue, combined with a good dose of human interest is what sets Amazing Stories *apart."*
Pamela Klaffke, *Calgary Herald*

AMAZING STORIES®

BILLY BISHOP TOP CANADIAN FLYING ACE

Dan McCaffery

MILITARY HISTORY

James Lorimer & Company Ltd., Publishers
Toronto

James Lorimer & Company Ltd., Publishers acknowledge the support of the Ontario Arts Council. We acknowledge the support of the Government of Canada through the Book Publishing Industry Development Program (BPIDP) for our publishing activities. We acknowledge the support of the Canada Council for the Arts for our publishing program. We acknowledge the support of the Government of Ontario through the Ontario Media Development Corporation's Ontario Book Initiative.

ONTARIO ARTS COUNCIL
CONSEIL DES ARTS DE L'ONTARIO

Canada Council
for the Arts

Library and Archives Canada Cataloguing in Publication

McCaffery, Dan
Billy Bishop top Canadian flying ace / Dan McCaffery

(Amazing stories)
ISBN 978-1-55277-413-7

1. Bishop, William A., 1894-1956. 2. Fighter pilots—Canada—Biography
3. Great Britain. Royal Flying Corps—Biography. 4. World War,
1914-1918—Aerial operations, British.
I. Title. II. Series: Amazing stories (Toronto, Ont.)

UG626.2.B5 M33 2009   940.4'4941092   C2009-900647-2

James Lorimer & Company Ltd., Publishers
317 Adelaide Street West, Suite 1002
Toronto, Ontario
M5V 1P9
www.lorimer.ca

Printed and bound in Canada

Contents

Prologue

Billy Bishop was tired of war.

Mentally and physically exhausted, when he looked in the mirror he saw a fat old man with a bulbous red nose and a head of thinning white hair. He had just turned 50, but he looked and felt 20 years older. The handsome, dashing young air ace of his youth had disappeared long ago.

Sitting in front of his typewriter on this cold spring day in 1944, the retired air marshal was surrounded by trophies from a career that had brought him fame and fortune. Mounted on a wall in front of him was the propeller from the Nieuport 17 fighter plane that had carried him through so many harrowing dogfights over the Western Front more than a quarter of a century earlier. Beside him lay the bullet-shattered windscreen from the same aircraft. He remembered the day that it had been punctured. A German pilot had sneaked up behind him, sending a hail of bullets whizzing just past his head. One had grazed his leather flying helmet before breaking the glass shield in front of his face. He still shuddered when he thought about that day.

Indeed, his dreams were still haunted from time to time by the many things he'd seen and done during three action-packed tours of duty all those years ago.

The walls of his study were covered with other keepsakes, including framed maps of the battlefields he'd flown over as a young man and photos of himself with everyone from British Prime Minister Winston Churchill to German Luftwaffe chief Hermann Goering.

In the closet hung his bright blue Royal Canadian Air Force uniform, which was adorned with almost every decoration a citizen of the British Empire could win, including the coveted Victoria Cross, two Distinguished Service Orders, the Military Cross, the Distinguished Flying Cross, two foreign gallantry awards, a stripe he'd earned for being wounded in action and three campaign medals. He'd won them for a career in which he was credited with downing 72 German planes and three observation balloons.

In all, he had spent 10 years of his life in uniform, counting his time as a cadet at the Royal Military College, his service as a fighter pilot in the Great War and his Second World War recruiting activities.

But now the fabled war hero was disillusioned. He'd travelled to London, where he'd seen the carnage Nazi bombers had inflicted on the civilian population. In the newspapers he'd read gloating accounts of Allied air attacks on German cities, including one in which 1,000 bombers had flattened Cologne in a single night. Now there was word that the Americans had developed a gigantic bomber known as the 'Superfortress.' In the Third Reich, meanwhile, Adolf Hitler had begun unleashing rockets on the United Kingdom.

On a nearby bookshelf sat Bishop's 1918 autobiography, Winged Warfare. *He hadn't looked at it in a long time because — as he frankly admitted to a reporter — it turned his stomach. Beside it was a novel,* The Flying Squad, *which he had co-authored back in 1927. It contained embarrassing anti-Jewish drivel, with which he was now ashamed to be associated. He'd seen what bigotry could lead to.*

Bishop placed his hands on the typewriter keys and began pounding out a paragraph for his new book, which he planned to call Winged Peace. *"We have all been brought up along narrow lines of nationalism and racism," he wrote. "As children we have been taught in the schools, and at the present time are teaching our own children, narrow and bigoted ideas about the rest of mankind."*

Bishop did believe that this war was worth fighting. Indeed, he'd ruined his health by working 18 hours a day to help build the Royal Canadian Air Force into one of the world's most powerful fighting machines. He knew the Nazis could only be stopped by brute force and he'd thrown himself into the task. But he knew, too, that this was the second global conflict in his lifetime. When his generation had gone off to fight in 1914, he'd been anxious to do his part. It was, after all, being called "the war to end all wars." But just 21 years after the shooting had stopped, another world war had broken out.

This war was not over yet, and it had already been far bloodier than the first. Making matters even more worrisome was the fact that Bishop's own children were in uniform. His daughter, Jackie, was an RCAF radio operator and his son, Arthur, was flying extraordinarily dangerous combat missions over France in a Spitfire fighter plane.

Perhaps this war was justified. But Bishop knew there had to be a better way for nations to resolve their differences. Steps had to be taken in future to head off wars before they started. He began typing another sentence: "If we do not leave World War II behind us determined that never again will man take up arms against his brother," it read, "may God help us."

The war hero had become a crusader for peace.

Chapter One
Early Life

William Avery Bishop came into the world in the little town of Owen Sound, Ontario, Canada on February 8, 1894.

The fair-haired, blue-eyed infant was born into an upper-middle-class family prominent in the affairs of Grey County. His father, Will, was a successful lawyer and the county registrar; his mother, Margaret, the daughter of a respected local doctor. Will Bishop was a dandy. He dressed in tailored suits, striped pants, silk shirts, leather boots, bow-tie and top hat. He was also a demanding, uncompromising man who was determined to get ahead in the world. And he did just that, building his family a splendid, three-storey Victorian home that still stands today on Owen Sound's Third Street. Will and Margaret had a daughter and three sons, including Billy, who was the second youngest of the four children. Interestingly, considering the way that Billy would make his name, his grandfather, Eleazar Bishop, was a German leather maker.

Right from the start, Billy was a youngster of awesome

contradictions. He spoke with a lisp, played the piano, preferred the company of girls and dressed for school in a suit
and tie. His hometown newspaper, the Owen Sound *Sun*,
painted a picture of a well-mannered young boy when it
reported: "a concert was given at the residence of Mr. W.
A. Bishop on Saturday afternoon last. An excellent musical
and literary program was carried out and a speech filled to
overflowing with good humour was delivered by little Billy
Bishop."

But Billy was no sissy. In fact, he enjoyed hunting and
horseback riding and was forever getting into schoolyard
fights. In athletics he had no time for hockey, lacrosse, base-
ball or any of the other popular team sports of the era, preferring instead such solitary pursuits as swimming and running.
Later, as a fighter pilot on the Western Front, he would be the
same way, shunning formation flying in favour of so-called
"lone-wolf" patrols.

He was an adventuresome child almost from the start.
Indeed, the Owen Sound *Sun* reported in 1904 that 10-year-
old Billy had built a toy airplane that could soar 160 feet into
the air. The machine, which he put together just one year
after the Wright brothers had flown the world's first airplane
at Kitty Hawk, North Carolina, was "a real credit to the inven-
tive mind of this lad," the paper said. Not content with that
achievement, Billy slapped together a rickety contraption
made of cardboard, wooden crates and string and hauled
it onto the roof of the family's home. Here, 30 feet off the

ground, he made his first solo flight. When his sister, Louie, dug him out of the wreckage he was, miraculously, unhurt. It was his first crash landing but it would by no means be his last.

In his teens, Billy was a poor student who often skipped class to hang out in the pool hall downtown. But he had a winning personality that made him popular with teachers and students alike. At 5 feet 6 inches he was short, even for the era, but he was a handsome young man: slim, with a firm jaw, full mouth, straight nose and a head of bushy blond hair. He had no trouble attracting female company, partly because of his good looks and charisma, but also because he was an incorrigible flirt.

One of the first to come under his spell was Margaret Burden, a dark-haired beauty he met when he was 16 years old. The granddaughter of department store magnate Timothy Eaton, Margaret was a Toronto girl who was summering on Georgian Bay with her family when she met Billy. For both of them it was love at first sight. Writer Alan Hynd, who interviewed the couple years later, wrote: "Billy was an outdoor boy, and he used to point out to her gaily coloured birds that a little girl never saw in the city. She talked about him so much that the two families eventually became acquainted. Fall came, and she went away. But she didn't forget, and neither did Billy."

In fact, young Bishop announced to his startled parents that he would marry Margaret some day. Unfortunately,

Margaret's father, who had married into wealth himself, disapproved of Bishop and would do everything in his power to break them up.

Meanwhile, Billy's grades continued to suffer. They were so mediocre that when he graduated from high school, university was simply out of the question. So his parents packed him off to cadet school, where admission standards were much lower. "I had never given much thought to being a soldier, even after my parents had sent me to the Royal Military College at Kingston, when I was seventeen years of age," he wrote in his autobiography. "I will say for my parents that they had not thought much of me as a professional soldier either. But they did think, for some reason or other, that a little military discipline at the Royal Military College would do me a lot of good — and I suppose it did."

To say that Billy failed to prosper at RMC would be putting it mildly. In an entrance exam, he came in 42nd out of the 43 students who were accepted. And worse was yet to come. As the end of his first year approached, he found himself unprepared for final exams. In a desperate move, he cheated, was caught and received a failing grade. Forced to repeat the year, he did much better, finishing 23rd out of 42 students. But the next year he was back to his old ways, muddling through in 33rd place out of 34 cadets, barely finishing ahead of the one young man who failed.

Billy's lack of academic success had a lot more to do with disinterest than it did with intelligence. The editor of the school's yearbook was perceptive enough to realize that. In the spring of 1913 he wrote: "About a week before the final exams a great change comes over our William. He no longer dallies with Amaryllis in the shade, but shilly-shallies with maths into the small hours of the morning. Having made up his mind to pass, he usually gets there, as he does with every-thing when put to it."

The truth is that Billy didn't care for RMC, which was noted in those days for its harsh discipline. He was late for parade. He failed to pass inspection. He snuck out after dark to go partying in Kingston. One evening, Bishop and a buddy broke curfew and stole a canoe in a bid to meet a pair of girls in town. Both young men had been drinking and, almost inevitably, they capsized and were caught. Billy was confined to barracks for a month for that infraction. His conduct was so notorious that the yearbook editor dedicated a full page to his shenanigans. And this entry suggests that some of his problems had to do with an obsession with girls:

> *Voice from cadet with telescope peering out of his window: "There's a red coat on Fort Henry hill. There's an umbrella too with a couple of people behind it. Wonder who it can be?" Voice from the next room: "Come on, Steve, Bill Bishop is out. Let's swipe his tobacco."*

The world will never know whether Bishop would have graduated from his final year, which was slated to begin in September 1914. The First World War broke out in August and

Billy, eager for adventure and glory, left RMC to join a cavalry regiment. Despite his poor record as a cadet, he was immediately given the rank of lieutenant. This was not as strange as it may sound today. Tens of thousands of young men were enlisting, most of them had no military training of any kind and there were not enough officers in the regular army to even begin to handle the sudden influx of soldiers. Billy, who could ride, shoot and march, was a notch above most of the newcomers.

Before heading off to training camp with the Seventh Canadian Mounted Rifles in London, Ontario, he stopped at the Burden home in Toronto and proposed to Margaret. Her father was still hostile to the idea of his daughter marrying beneath her social station, but she accepted his ring. "I just pray the war will not last too long," she said.

With that, Billy Bishop was off to war.

Chapter Two
The Road to War

If Bishop thought the war was going to be one big rollicking adventure, he was in for a rude shock. The training was hard and more than a little dangerous. On one cross-country exercise, he told Margaret in a letter, his horse reared up and fell on top of him, breaking his nose and two ribs. "It is really a wonder it didn't crush me to death," he confided. "I'm all stuck up in plasters and my right hand is sprained." But he was back in action three weeks later, setting a division record when he led his men through a four-mile march in a scant 42 minutes.

Days later, he nearly lost an eye when a rifle he was shooting backfired, sending the bolt crashing painfully into his cheekbone. Then there was the weather, which was exceptionally cold during that winter of 1915. "We slept here last night and cold, oh darling cold isn't the word for it," he wrote to his fiancée after spending a night in a barn. "Although wrapped up in three blankets we were all nearly frozen. It was so cold that we couldn't sleep at times and lay there telling each other just how cold we were."

Still, Bishop was developing into a good soldier. Corporal George Stirrett, who trained with him in London, remembered Billy as an excellent shot and a skilled horseman. He was so good, in fact, that he was made a machine-gun instructor and placed in charge of horseback training. He was helped, too, by the fact that the regiment's commander, Colonel Ibbotson Leonard, was a fellow RMC man. More than that, Leonard was an old friend of Billy's older brother, Worth Bishop. Not surprisingly, he soon took a shine to Bishop, often inviting the young soldier over to his quarters for dinner.

Bishop would eventually become famous as a killer of men, but his letters from this period show that he had a gentle side too. When word came in June that the regiment was to sail for England, he went out of his way to calm the fears of his loved ones. In a letter to Margaret, he wrote: "I am indeed the luckiest man in all the world. Nobody could possibly be luckier, and all due to you, my sweetheart. A man could do a lot in the world with a girl like you to inspire him." He also took care not to worry his parents unduly. Again writing to Margaret, he confided: "Mom and Dad go back this afternoon. I am not letting on to them that I won't see them again and have told them that it will probably be a month before we go. When we do go, Worth is merely going to telegraph them that I have gone, as we think that will be the easiest way."

Stirrett commented on his humanity too, noting that

Bishop mingled casually with the lower ranks, refusing to put on airs. "Bish was a nice fellow for an officer," he recalled in a 1981 interview. "He treated us more like buddies than subordinates. He'd laugh and joke with us. We slept in a drafty barn and, one night, he reached into the straw and pulled out a bottle of brandy and shared it with us. Maybe it was because he was the youngest officer in the camp, but he was well liked by the fellows who had to take orders from him."

On June 6, 1915, Bishop boarded a stinking old cattle ship called the *Caledonia*, and sailed for England. He never forgot the send-off the soldiers received at dockside from an adoring crowd of civilians. "As we pulled out of Montreal the crowds cheered and waved like mad," he wrote home. "Every whistle within miles blew furiously and our men sang *God Save the King* and cheered back. It was very impressive." It was also a little sad. "My heart swells when I think in a few hours we will see the last of Canada," he added. Before long, homesickness was the least of his worries. As the ship made its way into the rough North Atlantic, it was greeted by high seas that left most of the 240 men and all 600 horses on board severely seasick. Several animals died each day and their carcasses were heaved over the side. Near Ireland, German U-boats attacked the convoy, sending a couple of ships to watery graves. Somehow, the *Caledonia* got through, sailing into Plymouth on June 23.

At first, Bishop was thrilled to be in England, believing he was finally in the war zone. But before long the weather on the island's southeast coast was getting him down. In a letter to Margaret on July 7, he described a sandstorm that was so fierce the soldiers could barely breathe or open their eyes: "Even goggles are no protection. The fine sand gets in. Our eyes are all full of blood and the sand is so bad that some of the men's faces are bleeding."

On July 23 the camp was hit by driving rains. "We were soaked from head to toe and not a happy bunch," he told his fiancée. "We got to Canterbury about 6 and after fixing up the horses went into town to get a little dry, which was an impossibility. We slept in the open in our wet clothes and perhaps you can guess what we felt like this morning, especially as it started to rain again. I can hardly move a limb today."

One of Bishop's biographers has suggested that Billy was a chronic complainer who exaggerated the situation in a bid to win sympathy. The official history of the Canadian Expeditionary Force, he pointed out, described the summer as a dry one that presented no hardship to the men in the tents. Perhaps there was no discomfort for the bureaucrat who wrote the official history from the refuge of headquarters, but according to Corporal George Stirrett, who was with Bishop at this time, conditions in southern England were wet, damp and windy, "just about every damn time they sent us out to slop about on the horse lines."

The weather was so bad that Bishop decided to try to get out of the regiment. "By the time I had been there a month it seemed to me I had never seen anything but mud," he wrote in his 1944 book, *Winged Peace.* "I would stand fetlock deep in it in the horse lines looking up as the occasional airplane passed overhead, saying to myself, 'What a grand clean way to go to war.' Right then I decided to find out how a man went about the business of getting away from horses, baled hay, and mud — in short, how he acquired wings."

He applied for permission to join the Royal Flying Corps and was told there was a place for him in that fledgling service. But there was a catch. The RFC had plenty of pilots, he was informed, but not enough observers. They were the people who took aerial photos of enemy positions, observed German troop movements, dropped bombs and directed artillery fire. The observer, in short, was the guy who did all the work, while the pilot got most of the glory. If he was going to fight in the sky, Bishop was going to have to start out as the low man on the totem pole.

But as far as Billy was concerned, there was no alternative. He knew that trench warfare had made the cavalry obsolete. If he stayed with his regiment, he'd find himself assigned to a muddy, rat-infested trench on the Western Front. He would be expected to endure poison-gas attacks, constant bombardments and the occasional foot charge into the teeth of German machine guns. Bishop had already met wounded veterans who had warned him to stay away from the Front for as long as possible. The war was less than two years old and both sides had already lost hundreds of thousands of men. In any case, he spent the next several months training to be an observer with

21 Squadron at Netheravon Flight School. Here he proved to be a first-class observer. In fact, by the time he left, Bishop was in charge of training new observers with the camera.

He loved flying from the get-go. "This is the greatest game in the world, every minute full of intense excitement," he wrote home. "A man ceases to be a human when he is away up. The earth is merely a map and you feel that nothing is impossible." But going up in those primitive open-cockpit biplanes was exceptionally dangerous, as he was soon to find out. The machines were fragile and their motors unreliable. And there were no parachutes, because the high command feared the airmen might bail out rather than attempt to bring damaged airplanes home. Engines would conk out for no apparent reason, forcing the pilot to glide in for a forced landing on whatever terrain lay below. Bishop and his pilot, Roger Neville, survived more than a few forced landings, along with a couple of crash landings. In any case, in January 1916, 21 Squadron headed for France.

The timing of this posting, which seemed so inconsequential when it was announced, would be the first in a series of controversies that would haunt Bishop's reputation throughout his flying career. In his book *The Making of Billy Bishop*, the late Brereton Greenhous claimed that, as Billy did not arrive at the Front until 1916, he was not eligible to receive a campaign medal known as the 1914-1915 Star. Greenhous, in fact, claims that Billy shamelessly awarded the honour to himself. He wrote:

Only those officers and men who saw service in a theatre of war before 31 December 1915 would subsequently be entitled to wear the 1914–1915 Star. That meant, of course, that Bishop's former comrades in the cavalry made the cut, while he missed out by a matter of two and a half weeks. A form letter in his National Archives of Canada file confirms as much, listing the various campaign medals he was entitled to as a member of the Canadian Expeditionary Force and as an officer of the RFC and the RAF. Both British and Canadian authorities crossed out the 1914–1915 Star while acknowledging that he was eligible for the British War Medal and the Victory Medal. However, an examination of his tunic, now in the hands of the Canadian War Museum, reveals a 'red, white and blue, shaded and watered' ribbon in the appropriate place among the multitude of medals that adorn it. At some point in his later career Bishop unobtrusively awarded himself the 1914–1915 Star!

However, the Veterans Affairs Canada website states that: "The 1914–1915 Star was awarded to all who saw service in any theatre of war against the Central Powers between 05 August 1914 and 31 December 1915 except those eligible for the 1914 Star. Canada considered 'overseas' to be service beyond the three-mile limit."

In other words, going by the criteria set by the Canadian government, if a serviceman was sent beyond Canada's territorial waters during the time period in question, he qualified for the decoration. Bishop, who had made it all the way to England by June 1915, had travelled 2,297 miles farther than he needed to be eligible for the Star.

There's also the question of how Bishop could have awarded the decoration to himself, even if he had wanted to. Where would he even have found such a medal? They certainly weren't for sale anywhere. Did he make his own home-made version? We might also ask why anyone with seven gallantry awards and two other campaign medals to his name would bother to fake having won the 1914–1915 Star. It was a very minor award that was handed out to more than 2.3 million men. A more likely explanation is that Bishop had mistakenly been turned down for the decoration during the war, then successfully reapplied for it, perhaps many years later.

Any way you slice it, he *deserved* the medal. He had, after all, been aboard a convoy that was attacked by German submarines just off the coast of Ireland in June 1915. He had also spent that summer and fall in southern England, which was being visited on a regular basis by enemy airships. Indeed, German Zeppelins made 20 raids on the United Kingdom in 1915, killing 185 people and wounding 471 more. Bishop was, in a very real sense, in a war zone long before he got to France.

In any case, he was about to go into action aboard the

RE7, a lumbering two-seater that was quite possibly the worst warplane ever built. In a 1984 letter to the author, Roger Neville described it as a hopeless aeroplane. It could manage a top speed of only 60 miles per hour and had a tendency to stall at 45. Sitting in the front seat, Bishop couldn't figure out for the life of him how to defend the aircraft with the two Lewis machine guns that were at his disposal. "It will always remain a question of reasonable doubt whether anybody could have fired the gun at an enemy," he wrote later. "To have done so would have entailed possession of the eye of a sharpshooter and the agility of an acrobat, because to fire a bullet into the clear you first had to shoot through the maze of wires between the upper and lower wings, which gave the RE7 the appearance of a bird cage."

He never forgot his first foray into enemy territory. Bishop and Neville climbed to 10,000 feet before heading for the German lines. "There I had my first taste of ack-ack fire and I remember it was hard to take, though later I felt completely a hero for having come through this visit to the baptismal font of war," Billy wrote. "True, it was nothing like the anti-aircraft fire today's fliers endure. Its shooting was done by fallible human beings, not by scientific range-finding devices. But it was just as hard to take, for remember our machines were not so good either."

Wounded in Action

On one patrol, Bishop was grazed in the head by a piece of

shrapnel. Brereton Greenhous suggested in his book that Billy may have lied about the injury in a bid to win a "wound stripe." There was, he noted, no blood, only a bruise to the Canadian's head. But in a hand-written 1984 letter to this author, Roger Neville confirmed that Billy had indeed been hit by anti-aircraft fire. "Although I was not only his pilot but also his flight commander, he had no hesitation in blaming me for not dodging the missile," he wrote. "But we remained good friends."

Over the four months they were in combat together, the two men shared a number of harrowing experiences that made them almost as close as brothers. Once, the aircraft were ordered stripped of their guns so they could carry more bombs! They were then sent 18 miles behind enemy lines to bomb a railroad station. Fortunately, they made it there and back without encountering any German planes.

Bishop, who has often been painted as a "man without fear," in fact found the stress of these missions hard to take. After one flight behind enemy lines he wrote home: "In the air you feel only intense excitement. You cheer and laugh and keep your spirits up. You are all right just after you have land-ed as you search your machine for bullet and shrapnel holes. But two hours later when you are quietly sitting in your billet you feel a sudden loneliness. You want to lie down and cry."

But he kept his nerve, even after the RE7's engine cut out on takeoff, sending the machine plummeting to the ground. It finished "tail-up" in a farmer's field and Bishop's knee was seriously injured. "We had three 112-pound bombs on board but they did not explode," Neville recalled. "Bish was much more concerned about his damaged knee, which probably would not have been so damaged if he had obeyed regulations and been properly strapped in at take-off. But characteristically Bish was never one to take more notice of regulations than Horatio Nelson did."

Billy refused to seek medical attention, insisting he could remain on active duty, even with one gimpy leg. But after he fell off a gangplank while going ashore for leave that May, he was hospitalized for an indefinite period.

While he was recovering, Bishop had the good luck to meet Lady St. Helier, a wealthy, well-connected 69-year-old who spent much of her time in London's hospitals tending to the sick and wounded. Before long, she was pulling strings that would make his advancement a lot easier. She even arranged for him to be sent home to Canada on extended leave. When he returned to the United Kingdom in September, he applied for pilot training. With Lady St. Helier knocking down all obstacles, he was accepted.

He never forgot his first solo flight, and recalled it later: "An ambulance stood in the aerodrome, and it seemed to me, as it has to many another student-pilot, that all the other business of flying had suddenly ceased so that everybody could look at me. I noticed with a shiver that the ambulance had its engine running. Were the doctors at the hospital expectantly fondling their knives? Everybody looked cold-blooded and heartless. But I had to do it: so into the machine I crawled, trying to look cheerful, but feeling awfully lonesome. How I got off the ground I do not know, but once in the air it was not nearly so bad — not much worse than the first time you started down-hill on an old-fashioned bicycle."

From the very beginning he was a lone wolf who preferred to fly off by himself. "I hate formation flying," he wrote home. I'm always expecting to have collisions and that is a nasty thought. We fly in a group only about 25 feet from each other."

Bishop soon found out just how dangerous flight training could be. After a particularly rough day spent flying the Avro 504 trainer, he wrote home:

> *Yesterday I had three forced landings on them, two of which I managed to get into the aerodrome, but the last one I crashed on the side of a hill, not very badly, nobody was hurt and the machine is repairable. The engines are so very unreliable in them.*
>
> *Last night we had a boy killed here and another in my squadron this morning. I saw them both, perfectly ghastly sights. The one today was on a Sopwith. He was diving it and the wings fell off. The thing fell like a stone 3,000 feet, the poor beggar struggling all the time, helpless. Then they killed a pupil at Netheravon today also, so we aren't doing too badly, are we?*
>
> *Those things used to upset me so horribly, but now I think I have become an*

> *absolute firmly believing fatalist and they*
> *don't worry my nerves in the least. If I am*
> *for it, then I am, and nothing can save me;*
> *but I firmly believe I am NOT for it.*

But even this "devil-may-care" attitude couldn't shield Bishop forever from the stress of making daily flights in unreliable machines. "I find that flying wears frightfully on one's nerves and a few days absolutely away from it does a world of good," he wrote home in late September 1916.

Somehow, he survived his training, winning his wings that November. After that, he was posted to 37 Squadron at Northholt, where he would spend the next few months hunting for Zeppelins in the dark and dangerous skies over London.

Night flying! It was quite possibly the most harrowing job a fighting man faced during the First World War. He found himself flying in pitch darkness, without radar or other navigational aids that modern pilots take for granted, dodging British anti-aircraft fire and straining to find the elusive airships in the dim white searchlights. "I don't know of many greater tests of a pilot's skill than this flying in the dark, with a lot of machines about you in the air; their little navigation lights looking for all the world like so many moving stars," he wrote. "The cold of the higher altitudes at night is agonizingly intense. After half an hour or so in the frigid zone you get some sort of numb and then for a long while the cold doesn't seem to affect you any more. The real nasty part is when you have landed and begin to thaw out. It is really worse than the original freezing."

Phantom Combat?

Bishop never did find a Zeppelin, but on January 7, 1917 he claimed his first encounter with the enemy, a claim that would later cause controversy once again. In a letter home, he wrote: "I spent the day taking mechanics for joy rides, and then just about noon a Hun seaplane toddled over, and Headquarters ordered me to go up after him. I did and caught up to him at 1,000 feet and had a terrific scrap. He had an observer and I was alone but I was in a BE12a and it was very fast. I must have hit him over and over again but didn't finish him. He hit my machine six times — three times, funny to say, in the propeller."

Bishop's logbook makes no mention of a dogfight that day, leading at least one critic, Brereton Greenhous, to accuse him of making up a story to impress his loved ones. But German seaplanes *were* raiding the coast at that time. In his book *The Sky on Fire*, author Raymond H. Fredette wrote: "Quite regularly since 1914, single-engined German aero-planes had braved the Channel, one or two at a time, to drop a few bombs along the coast. Their favourite target was Dover Harbour. After more than twenty such 'tip-and-run' attacks, the British had come to accept them as a routine nuisance."

If Bishop was going to make up a "war story," he could have done better than this. He did not claim to have shot his opponent down and could not even say for certain that he had scored any hits on it. And he frankly admitted that his own plane had been damaged. At the very most, he was claiming to have taken part in an inconsequential standoff. Besides, in addition to mentioning six joyrides for mechanics, Bishop's log for the day in question also makes note of one 10-minute flight for an unspecified purpose. Could that have been the flight in which he chased off the seaplane?

The BE12a could reach an altitude of 3,000 feet in five minutes. Bishop claimed that he encountered the German at 1,000 feet, so presumably he could have reached that altitude in just a minute or two. If the enemy machine was nearby, he could have caught up to it very shortly after takeoff. Most aerial battles lasted less than a minute, so he may well have had enough time to engage the seaplane and get back to base within 10 minutes. And if the flight had actually lasted 12 or 13 minutes, he could well have simply rounded off the number to 10 when glancing at his watch after landing. There's also another possibility — that Bishop, for whatever reason, chose not to record the skirmish in his log. Whatever actually happened, there's no hard evidence that he invented the incident.

In any case, shortly after this event, he was ordered to report to 60 Squadron, which was stationed just nine miles behind the trenches at Arras. From now on he'd be meeting all the enemy planes he could handle.

Chapter Three
Bloody April

I t's doubtful if any novice fighter pilot in history was sent into action at a more perilous time and place than those Billy Bishop faced in the spring of 1917. He reported to 60 Squadron, which was based at Filescamp Farm aerodrome, not far from Vimy Ridge, on March 9, just as the Royal Flying Corps was about to enter the darkest period in its history. On the surface, things did not look too bleak. The squadron, which consisted of three flights of six planes each, had one of the best records in the RFC. And it was equipped with the Nieuport 17, a small, sleek, French-built single-seat biplane that was fast and manoeuvrable.

Bishop was impressed with his new mount. "Being a French model the Nieuport Scout is a beautiful creature," he wrote. "The distinctly British machines — and some of our newer ones are indeed marvels of the air — are built strictly for business, with no particular attention paid to the beauty of the lines. The French, however, never overlook such things." But the Nieuport had its drawbacks. For one, it was a fragile aircraft that tended to shed its top wing in a steep dive. For another, it came equipped with just one weapon — a Lewis machine gun mounted on the top wing so that its bullets could clear the propeller blade.

On the other side of the trenches, the Germans were flying the new Albatros D-3, a torpedo-shaped biplane equipped with an interrupter gear that allowed its two machine guns to fire through its own whirling prop without hitting its blades. And being partially made of plywood, it was a much sturdier plane, capable of taking a lot more punishment than the Nieuport. Making matters worse was the fact that Germany's top fighter squadron, *Jasta 11*, commanded by Baron Manfred von Richthofen, was located directly across the front lines from 60 Squadron. Richthofen, who had painted his entire Albatros bright red, was known to both friend and foe as the Red Baron. He had almost 30 Allied planes to his credit, making him the leading living ace on either side. Most of his pilots were also exceptionally skilled.

But if Bishop was afraid, he didn't let on. In a letter home he wrote: "I'm very keen for a scrap in the air for I feel quite confident that I shall be able to take care of myself alright with a machine gun. That sounds conceited, doesn't it? But I didn't mean it that way."

Bishop got his chance to prove himself on March 25, 1917 when 60 Squadron's commander, Major Jack Scott, led four Nieuports across enemy lines just before sunset. They droned along uneventfully for some time before all hell broke loose. A trio of green- and mauve-coloured Albatros D-3s roared in behind them, rapidly closing the distance between the two formations. Scott turned the Nieuport flight around just in time to meet the Germans head on and a wild dogfight ensued.

That night, in a dugout 300 yards from the front line, Bishop described the heart-stopping encounter in a letter to Margaret: "Four of us were doing a patrol when we encountered three Huns. I hit mine, I think, for he suddenly fell out of control and I dove after him. I must have been going over 200 miles an hour so you can imagine how fast he was falling. I poured another 60 bullets at him and followed him vertically downwards from 8,000 feet to 600 feet." At that point his engine oiled up and stopped. Bishop was 600 feet over "no man's land," the territory between the opposing trenches, and he glided into a field that had only been captured two days earlier. "It was a narrow squeak," he added. "I tried to start my engine again but it refused, so I am stuck here for the night. I am so anxious to know if the Hun really crashed, for if he did he will count as one machine for me."

Bishop had nothing to worry about in that regard. The crew of a British anti-aircraft battery located just behind the Front had witnessed the fight and confirmed the kill. Jack Scott was so impressed that he made the young Canadian a flight commander.

It would prove a tragic mistake, for victory or no victory, Billy Bishop didn't have the experience or the temperament to be a good leader. He proved that a few days later when he led his patrol into an ambush near Vitry. A gaggle of Albatroses jumped them from out of the sun, shooting two of the Nieuports down. One pilot, Lieutenant William Garnett, was killed instantly. The other, 19-year-old Frank Bower, managed to nurse his battered machine over to the Allied side of the lines before making an emergency landing. He climbed out of the cockpit with his intestines hanging out, collapsed and died. The other four Nieuports only escaped by diving into a cloudbank.

More calamities awaited Bishop on March 31, when his flight was ordered to escort a group of BE two seaters on a reconnaissance mission. Once again a swarm of Albatroses pounced on them and two more Allied planes were lost, including one of the two-seaters and a Nieuport flown by E. J Townsend, a pilot who had gone to RMC with Billy. But this time Bishop managed to exact some revenge when he went to the assistance of another Nieuport that was being attacked, blowing one of the attackers out of the sky. "I opened fire twice, the last time at 50 yards range," he wrote in his combat report. "My tracers were seen to hit his machine in the centre section. The Albatros seemed to fall out of control, as he was in a spinning nose dive with his engine on. H.A. [hostile aircraft] crashed at 7:30 a.m."

Attached to this report was a note from Lieutenant B. A. Leckie, who wrote: "I was behind Lieutenant Bishop and saw the Albatros Scout go down in a spinning nose dive, seemingly out of control." Major Scott added that Bishop's victim had been seen to crash by British anti-aircraft batteries.

The Military Cross

As the airmen on opposing sides engaged in these duels, the Canadian Corps was getting ready to storm Vimy Ridge. In a bid to prevent the Germans from observing preparations for this historic assault, the Allies tried desperately to shoot down enemy observation balloons in the area. The balloons were tethered at an altitude anywhere from 1,000 to 3,000 feet by wire cables. Their observers, dangling from wicker baskets just under the gasbags, had a bird's-eye view behind Allied lines.

On the surface, they might appear easy targets. They were big and stationary, and they would often burst into flames after only a few rounds of ammunition had been pumped into them. But the balloons were heavily defended. Each one was guarded by anti-aircraft cannons and long-range machine guns. German fighters often patrolled nearby to provide further protection. For these reasons, most pilots dreaded attacking them.

Nevertheless, the balloons had to be taken out, and Bishop was assigned to attack one on April 7, 1917. He did just that, winning his first gallantry award in the process. As he dived at the hostile balloon, an Albatros scout engaged him from behind. "I turned and fired 15 to 20 rounds at 100 yards range," reads his combat report. "Tracers were seen going into his machine, he dived away steeply. I dived on the balloon, which was then on the ground, and opened fire at 800 feet, finishing my drum when approximately fifty feet above it. Nearly all of the bullets entered the balloon and black smoke was visible coming out of it in two places."

There were no witnesses to this feat, but there is no reason to doubt Bishop's story. He was modest in his report. He made no claim that the German fighter had crashed or that the balloon had gone up in flames. Nevertheless, Major Scott gave Billy credit for two victories, which left him just one shy of the five triumphs needed to win the unofficial title of "ace."

In the days and weeks ahead, such generous score-keeping would become common practice in the Royal Flying Corps. Battered by staggering losses, the British decided to give their airmen credit for victories even when they had done nothing more than drive an enemy plane off.

In fact, there were four different victory categories in the RFC: *destroyed, driven down out of control (DOOC), driven down* and *forced to land*. Planes classified as *destroyed* were seen to crash, go down in flames or break up in the air. Those *DOOC* were spotted falling out of control but not actually seen to crash. Such machines were considered to be in their death dives, but in reality, that was seldom the case. When in trouble, German pilots would often drop into an intentional spin. Planes reported as *driven down* were seen to fall, apparently under at least partial control. Such aircraft may have been damaged but were almost never actually destroyed. Aircraft listed as *forced to land* were usually damaged, and their crewmen were often wounded, but they were definitely not destroyed.

This method of recording victories would prove good for morale, both among the fighter squadrons and on the home front, but it would eventually do a great deal of harm to Bishop's reputation.

Whether his latest two victims had been destroyed or not, Billy was in a buoyant mood when he wrote to Margaret that evening. "I think I am fairly certain of getting a decoration for it," he said. "Tonight the commanding general, RFC, wired my CO, 'Congratulate Lieut. Bishop on his fine feat today,' so I am very bucked with life tonight." He was right about the medal. A few days later word came that he had won the Military Cross.

An Ace Is Born

Bishop doubled his score on April 8, when he was credited with an astounding four victories. The day started well for the Canadian, who was part of a five-man morning patrol led by Major Scott. At 9:30 a.m. Scott and Bishop teamed up to shoot down a German two-seater, giving Billy his first "shared" victory and his third witnessed kill. A few minutes later the Ontario pilot went after a balloon, peppering it with tracers as it sagged to the ground. Although it failed to catch fire, he was credited with a "driven down" victory.

Before the morning was over he would be credited with two more Albatros D-3s, including one that he reported falling with its nose well down and another that went into a spinning nosedive. One of these machines may have been flown by Sebastian Festner of the Red Baron's squadron. It is known that Festner, one of Richthofen's rising young stars with five victories to his credit, was with a flight of Albatroses that collided with 60 Squadron that morning. Festner did, in fact, pull out of the dogfight after his lower port wing nearly came off. The German's plane had not been hit by enemy bullets so we can only conclude the damage was sustained as he took violent evasive action to avoid Bishop's fire. In any case, Billy appears to have been the pilot who forced Festner to withdraw. Richthofen noted in a report to his superiors that Festner's machine was being sent home as useless for combat.

In all, Bishop was credited that morning with one two-seater destroyed, one balloon driven down and two Albatroses sent down out of control. The two-seater was shared with Scott, so we know that victory was witnessed. As for the other three, the record is not clear. The late historian Brereton Greenhous has written that Jack Scott may have seen Bishop's two Albatroses go down himself, and he may be correct because the Englishman was right in the thick of the action. In any case, Bishop was now recognized as an ace and his mechanic, Walter Bourne, celebrated by painting the nose of Billy's Nieuport bright blue.

German planes now began falling before Bishop's gun like ninepins. Flying alone on April 20, he claimed to have shot a German two-seater down in flames. Although there were no Allied witnesses, Jack Scott gave him credit for this, his ninth victory.

Two days later, Bishop scored twice more. He was leading an offensive patrol when he spotted Major Scott 2,000 feet below him, under attack by five single-seaters. He dived to Scott's assistance. This time, five British pilots, including Scott, witnessed his handiwork. In his combat report, the Canadian described it like this: "I fired 15 rounds at one and he dived steeply, apparently damaged. I then attacked a second one from the flank and fired 20 rounds at him, most of the bullets apparently hitting his machine. He dove down through the clouds apparently out of control."

Bishop had pulled this ambush off brilliantly, very probably sending both his adversaries scurrying for home in damaged machines. Although it is doubtful whether either of them crashed, Scott was fully justified, under RFC rules, in crediting Bishop with his tenth and eleventh victories.

The Canadian added two more to his score on April 23. First, he attacked a two-seater that landed intact in a field behind German lines. A few minutes later, he picked off one of three Albatroses that were stalking a lone Nieuport far behind enemy lines.

A Controversial Dogfight

Bishop was given credit for his 14th victory on April 27 when he sent a balloon down smoking. Two days later, he scored

again, sending a Halberstadt fighter down in flames in front
of two Allied witnesses in a nearby FE2b two-seater.

The next day, April 30, 1917, Bishop and Jack Scott
clashed with four red Albatroses in what would go down in
Royal Flying Corps lore as one of the classic air battles of the
First World War. Afterward, the young Canadian was convinced he'd fought a duel with Manfred von Richthofen. In
his autobiography, he wrote:

> *The Major reached them first and opened*
> *fire on the rear machine from behind.*
> *Immediately the leader of the scouts did a*
> *lightning turn and came back at the Major,*
> *firing at him and passing within two or three*
> *feet of his machine. In my turn, I opened fire*
> *on the Baron, and in another half-moment*
> *found myself in the midst of what seemed*
> *to be a stampede of blood-thirsty animals.*
> *Everywhere I turned smoking bullets were*
> *jumping at me, and although I got in two*
> *or three good bursts at the Baron's 'red*
> *devil,' I was rather bewildered for two or*
> *three minutes, as I could not see what was*
> *happening to the major and was not at all*
> *certain as to what was going to happen*
> *to me.... Around and around we went in*
> *cyclonic circles for several minutes, here a*
> *flash of the Hun machines, then a flash of*
> *silver as my squadron commander would*
> *whiz by. It was a lightning fight, and I have*

never been in anything just like it.

The battle only ended when a flight of British Sopwith Triplanes showed up and the Germans retreated. For the next eight decades historians assumed that Bishop had clashed with Richthofen and three of his best men. But in an article for an American aviation journal, the late Phil Markham accused Bishop of making up the story of his fight with the Red Baron. Markham claimed that Richthofen did not fly on the day in question. In fact, he said the Baron had been ordered by the Kaiser not to fly on April 30. Richthofen had scored four kills on April 29, bringing his total to 52, and the German head of state wanted to meet him on May 2. Brereton Greenhous repeats Markham's claim in his book, stating emphatically: "We know Manfred von Richthofen did not fly at all on the last day of 'Bloody April.'"

In 2007, internationally recognized Richthofen expert Peter Kilduff waded into the debate. In his fifth book about Richthofen, *Red Baron: The Life and Death of an Ace*, he wrote that the fabled German pilot "very likely had a brief fight with Captain William A. Bishop, MC, then a 14-victory Canadian ace."

Kilduff later explained on an aviation history website known as the Aerodrome that "our understanding of everything that happened on any particular day during the war is imperfect due to a lack of complete German records (in this case, a missing *Jasta 11* war diary), and that we need to interpret events." So he had checked Richthofen's own account to see where the known facts pointed: "Sure enough, the 1920, uncensored, edition of Richthofen's memoirs stated very clearly that he did not leave for his meeting with the Kaiser until the morning of 1 May 1917. Since he left with very light luggage, he did not need a full day to pack for his meeting and he certainly had time for and interest in another flight. Thus, he would almost certainly have flown on 30 April in hopes of adding another victory to his credit and to observe Lothar (his younger brother) in his new role as acting Staffel [squadron] leader." Based on that assessment, Kilduff concluded that the encounter between Richthofen and Bishop appeared more likely.

It could be argued that Richthofen was not likely to disobey a direct order from the Kaiser. But he may have figured that if he got his 53rd kill, all would be forgiven. He had to know that the high command would not dare to court martial the country's most famous war hero. Besides, as Greenhous pointed out in a discussion about Jack Scott, First World War squadron commanders sometimes flew missions when ordered not to do so. After landing, they would list them in official records as "recreation" flights. Richthofen knew, too, that if he failed to score, higher authority would not even know he had left the ground. And if he were killed, it would hardly matter if he were in trouble with his superiors.

Whether Richthofen flew or not that day, there's no evidence that Bishop made up his story. Major Scott's combat report proves that he and Bishop did indeed take part in a tough fight with four Albatroses that afternoon. In fact, Scott admits that his plane was damaged and that he had a difficult time escaping from a skilfully flown Albatros. And in a letter to his fiancée, written just a few hours after the fight, Bishop wrote: "The CO and I went out and got mixed up with four really good Huns. We chased them away, but oh heavens, did they shoot well. Seven bullets went through my machine within six inches of me, and one within an inch."

Bishop knew that Richthofen's fighter squadron, *Jasta 11*, was operating directly across the lines from 60 Squadron. He knew also that a deadly marksman was leading the Germans he encountered that day. It was only natural for him to assume he'd collided with the legendary enemy ace. Indeed, the Red Baron seems to have spooked many Allied airmen throughout his career. After the war, a British gunner with 20 Squadron said, "My pilot thought every German pilot was von Richthofen."

Chapter *Four*
A Hardened Killer

illy Bishop closed out April 30, 1917 with two victories over German observation planes, shooting one down and forcing the other to land in a cow pasture behind enemy lines. The day's work gave him a total of 17 confirmed triumphs — 14 planes and three balloons — in just five weeks on the Front. It was an amazing performance for a novice pilot, and it made him the number two ace in the entire Royal Flying Corps. Only Englishman Albert Ball, with 36 planes to his credit, was ahead of him in the scoring sweepstakes.

What made the Canadian's record all the more remarkable was the fact that the rest of 60 Squadron — and the rest of the RFC for that matter — had taken a terrible drubbing during what would go down in history as "Bloody April." Indeed, Major Scott reported the loss of 10 of the squadron's 18 planes during one weekend that month. For the 30 days as a whole, the outfit lost 20 planes, a casualty rate of 110 per cent. The flying corps lost 245 aircraft and 319 men that month, or fully one-third of its entire strength. Things were so bad that the life expectancy for new pilots was now a scant 11 days.

So how had the inexperienced Canadian done so well so quickly? Emerson Smith, who went to school with Bishop at Owen Sound Collegiate before becoming a fighter pilot on the Western Front himself, gave one explanation in a 1965 interview with CBC Radio. "His big forte was shooting," Smith recalled. "He practiced shooting continuously, every moment you might say that he was out of his plane he was firing his machine gun. He was an expert at firing."

Roger Neville noticed the same thing at 21 Squadron, telling this author that Bishop was a very fine shot who spent hours on the range where armament was tested on the ground near the airfield, adjusting and firing his Lewis gun. "Bish was by no means the best observer in the squadron," he said, "but he was by far the best air gunner."

Fellow 60 Squadron pilot J. B. Crompton credited much of Bishop's success to his eyesight. In an interview after the war, Crompton marvelled at Billy's ability to spot enemy aircraft long before other members of the patrol had seen them.

But it was more than that. Bishop was also driven by a burning ambition to get ahead. He frankly admitted this in both his public and private writings, saying that he wanted to get a large number of Germans to his credit. And he drove himself tirelessly, once flying 10 patrols in two days. Few pilots flew that many missions in a week. He would lead his flight on two or three patrols per day, then go off on a couple of solo forays before the sun set.

William Molesworth, who flew with Bishop at 60 Squadron, was astonished by what he saw. In a letter home he noted that Bishop worked by himself a lot, preferring to surprise the enemy by hiding rather than by trying to get him in a scrap. "Wish I could do the same," he wrote. "I always feel so fagged after a patrol, that I haven't got the energy or the patience to sit up in the clouds waiting for a chance to bag a 'lone Hun.'"

There was yet another reason. Bishop had become addicted to combat. Jack Thomson, an author and war veteran himself, saw the same thing happen to many men. "Combat addiction is caused when during a firefight, the body releases a large amount of adrenaline into your system and you get what is referred to as a 'combat high,'" he wrote. "This combat high is like getting an injection of morphine — you float around, laughing, joking, having a great time, totally oblivious to the dangers around you. The experience is very intense if you live to tell about it. Problems arise when you begin to want another fix of combat, and another, and another, and before you know it, you're hooked."

In his autobiography, Bishop recalled sometimes laughing in the midst of extreme danger. "I would fly as much as seven-and-a-half hours a day," he added. "Far from affecting my nerves, the more I flew, the more I wanted to fly, the better I seemed to feel and each combat became more and more enjoyable."

In calmer moments, he tried to rationalize what he was

doing by telling himself it was not a business or a profession, but all a big game. "The excitement of the chase had a tight hold on my heartstrings, and I felt that the only thing I wanted to do was to stay right at it and fight and fight and fight in the air. I don't think I was ever happier in my life," he wrote in his autobiography. "It seemed that I had found the one thing I loved above all others."

But there was one other factor that made Bishop a high-scoring ace, and it may have been the most important one of all. He was a killer. And despite what we've all seen in scores of Hollywood movies, such men were the exception, not the rule.

In his groundbreaking book *On Killing*, soldier-scholar Dave Grossman presented startling evidence that most soldiers never fire their guns in combat. In fact, a comprehensive study of several thousand United States Army infantrymen conducted at the end of the Second World War found that only 15 to 20 per cent had used their weapons against the enemy.

"Those who did not fire did not run and hide," Grossman wrote. "In many cases they were willing to risk great danger to rescue comrades, get ammunition, or run messages, but they simply would not fire their weapons at the enemy. There is within most men an intense resistance to killing their fellow man. A resistance so strong that, in many circumstances, soldiers on the battlefield will die before they can overcome it."

Grossman found the same thing was true among pilots.

The United States Army Air Corps discovered that during the Second World War less than 1 per cent of its fighter pilots accounted for 30 to 40 per cent of all enemy aircraft destroyed in the air. It was not fear that prevented the other men from killing. These pilots bravely followed proven killers who took them into dangerous situations. "But when it came time to kill," he wrote, "they looked into the cockpit at another man, a pilot, a flier, one of the 'brotherhood of the air,' a man frighteningly like themselves; and when faced with such a man it is possible that the vast majority simply could not kill him."

That may well explain why, after shooting down his first plane, Bishop could write home, "I am now the only person in Number 60 who has brought down a Hun without help from other machines."

Grossman said that, after the end of the Second World War, when the United States Air Force examined the backgrounds of its aces to help in pre-selecting future fighter pilots, they could only find one common denominator: the aces had all been involved in a lot of fights as children. They were not bullies — who avoid fights with anyone who is reasonably capable of fighting them — but fighters. Certainly Bishop fell into this category, as his son, Arthur, makes clear in his book *The Courage of the Early Morning*. In one particularly memorable episode, Arthur recalled, Billy fought no less than seven other boys in a schoolyard scrap.

Grossman found that when soldiers and pilots do kill,

it's often because they've been taught to dehumanize their opponents: "If your propaganda machine can convince your soldiers that their opponents are not really human, but are 'inferior forms of life,' their natural resistance to killing their own species will be reduced," he wrote. "Often the enemy's humanity is denied by referring to him as a 'gook,' 'Kraut' or 'Nip.'" During the First World War, Allied servicemen were repeatedly told that the Germans were fiends who bayoneted babies in Belgium, bombed cities with Zeppelins, shot female spies, sank passenger liners filled with women and children and used poison gas. Bishop certainly picked up on this, continuously referring to his adversaries as 'Huns' in both his letters and his autobiography.

There's no doubt that Bishop was also motivated by anger. The Germans had slain dozens of his friends and were trying to kill him every day. In one of his letters home, he wrote, "My heart is full these days. We are having the most awful time. Yesterday, Binnie, a friend of mine and three others were shot down and today, four of my flight went under in a scrap. I'll make them pay for this, I swear I will."

Before long, Bishop was addicted not only to the excitement of combat, but also to the violence. We see this in his letters home. There are comments such as, "You have no idea how bloodthirsty I've become and how much pleasure I get in killing Huns." Or: "I shot down another balloon in flames and I think I killed the two people in the basket. It was great fun." Or, "Margaret, my machine, my new one, is a wonder. It fairly tears through the air. Tonight, just to celebrate it, I shot down a Pfalz in flames from 17,500 feet. There were four of them and I was so pleased to see a Hun again that I just had to try my gun on them. Sure enough, down they went, and one in flames. 'Twas a merry sight withal." After shooting his first plane down in flames, he wrote, "I must say that to see an enemy going down in flames is a source of great satisfaction. The moment you see the fire break out you know that nothing in the world can save the man, or men, in the doomed machine."

Of course he was by no means the only ace who grew to enjoy his trade. But his combination of fabulous marksmanship, burning ambition, addiction to danger and an ability to dehumanize his enemies made him a very formidable fighter pilot indeed.

The Distinguished Service Order

As May dawned, Bishop's victories continued to pile up. He downed a pair of two-seaters on the second of the month. One went into the books as destroyed, the other was listed as driven down out of control. He had no witnesses for either triumph, but Major Scott granted him confirmations for both. He also recommended Bishop for his second decoration, the coveted Distinguished Service Order, which was quickly granted. Two days later, Billy scored a controversial "shared" victory with Willie Fry, his deputy flight leader. The two airmen were eating lunch in the squadron mess when word came through that a German two-seater was in the vicinity, directing artillery fire on Allied troops. They took off at once, with Bishop leading.

In his combat report, the Canadian wrote: "With Lieut. Fry following me I dived at two two-seaters. I fired twenty rounds at one and turned off, Lieut. Fry diving on and firing. I dived again as he stopped firing and fired about forty rounds.... The machine did two turns of a spin and then nose dived to earth where we saw him crash. I fired a short burst at long range at the second one which flew away and did not return."

At the bottom of this report was a note that read, "I dived with Capt. Bishop and fired a long burst at close range at the same time as him. H.A. [hostile aircraft] spun and crashed W[est] of Brebieres." Although this annotation had the typewritten words 'Lieut. Fry' attached to it, there was no actual signature, a fact that was to create a major controversy almost eight decades later. In 1994, Fry would claim that he did not see the two-seater crash and had not written the comments attributed to him. This has led some to speculate that Bishop forged Fry's comments at the bottom of the combat report. However, on the day of the incident, Fry — in his own logbook — claimed a shared victory with Bishop! The entry reads: "1 H.A. brought down and crashed near Brebieres with Bishop."

We know this to be true because Fry himself tells us about the logbook entry in his 1974 autobiography, *Air of*

Battle. In the book, he expresses no doubts about the veracity of the victory. We must assume that his memory on the day of the dogfight was more reliable than his recollections almost 80 years after the fact.

The Leading Ace

Bishop's second victory that day was also witnessed by 60 Squadron pilot G. L. Lloyd. In a letter to this author, written in 1987, Canadian aviation historian Stewart Taylor quoted from an RFC document: "Lloyd, also on this patrol, could not get down to the HA in time, but saw one flatten out after diving to 2,000 feet and another going down completely out of control."

With that, Bishop left the Front for a two-week leave. He arrived in England in time to find out that Albert Ball — the leading British pilot, with 44 victories behind his name — had just been killed in action. Bishop, with 19 planes and three observation balloons to his credit, was now the top living ace of the Royal Flying Corps. It was a title he didn't intend to relinquish.

When he returned to action in late May, he quickly picked up where he had left off, claiming three victories before the month expired. None of them were witnessed but Jack Scott, who believed in Bishop explicitly, confirmed all three. Billy's score was rising, but he craved more decorations. Specifically, he wanted the Victoria Cross, the Empire's highest gallantry award. And he was cooking up a scheme that he thought just might win it for him. He hinted as much in a letter to Margaret on May 31, writing: "I have a great plan in mind. A real hair-raising stunt that I am going to try one of these days."

To his comrades he was more specific. At a mess party on the evening of June 1 he told his mates that he was going to attack a German airfield the next morning at dawn.

He planned, he said, to shoot the enemy pilots down one by one as they tried to take off to intercept him. Bishop asked pilots Keith Caldwell and Willie Fry to accompany him.

Caldwell refused and Fry was noncommittal. The next morning, Bishop awoke at 3:00 a.m. and again asked Fry to come along on the raid. This time, the Englishman turned him down flat.

Undaunted, Bishop took off by himself on what would become the most controversial mission in the history of aerial warfare.

Chapter Five

The Victoria Cross

illy Bishop crossed into German territory just as the sun was coming up. He swooped down on the airfield he had pre-selected, only to be greeted by a deafening silence. The place was deserted. Angry and disappointed, he flew a little further, hoping to find some soldiers to strafe. Suddenly, he stumbled upon another airfield. Below he could see six Albatros fighters and a two-seater lined up on the tarmac, some with their engines running. He had arrived just moments before the Germans were about to launch their dawn patrol.

In his combat report, he described what happened next:

I fired on seven machines on the aerodrome, some of which had their engines running. One of them took off and I fired 15 rounds at him from close range 60 feet up and he crashed. A second one taking off, I opened fire and fired 30 rounds at 150 yards range, he crashed into a tree. Two more were then taking off together. I climbed and engaged

*one at 1,000 feet, finishing my drum, and
he crashed 300 yards from the aerodrome. I
changed drums and climbed east. A fourth
H.A. came after me and I fired one whole
drum into him. He flew away and I then flew
1,000 feet under four scouts at 5,000 feet
for one mile and turned west climbing. The
aerodrome was armed with one or more
machine guns.*

Bishop arrived back at Filescamp Farm at 5:40 a.m., firing off red flares to signal to those below that he was returning in triumph. As his blue-nosed Nieuport came to a halt, a swarm of men gathered around it. One was Willie Fry. Recalling the scene later, he said he noticed that the plane's Lewis gun was missing and that there was a group of about five bullet holes in the rear half of his tailplane, in a circle not more than six inches in diameter.

Fry, in his old age, would tell researchers that he had seen powder burns around the holes. More than that, he said, Bishop told him that he had tossed his gun overboard because it had become stuck in a downward position on its Foster mount while he was changing ammo drums. Bishop also told him, Fry said, that he'd become lost on his way home and had landed in a field behind Allied lines to ask farmers for directions home.

To some, these statements could only mean one thing — Bishop had landed behind his own lines and shot up his own plane with his own gun, then flown home with a completely false tale of a single-handed attack on an enemy airfield. After the war, when piecemeal German records failed to corroborate any such raid, the doubts grew even deeper.

Assuming that Fry's recollections were accurate, there would not have been anything particularly sinister about two of his three claims. If Bishop's gun had indeed become stuck in a downward position it would have blocked his vision and presented a very real safety hazard in the event of a heavy landing. So there would have been good reason to throw it away. As for being on the ground before returning to base, there is nothing unusual or nefarious about that. Any pilot will admit that it is easy to become lost — even flying over territory you are familiar with — if you skim the treetops for any length of time.

However, powder burns around the bullet holes could only mean one thing — that the damage was inflicted on a stationary target by someone no more than three feet away.

But Bishop never mentioned — either in his combat report or his autobiography — landing behind Allied lines or returning without his gun. Nor should it be forgotten that research by Brereton Greenhous shows that every Royal Flying Corps squadron had to fill out a report each week on any lost machine guns. For the week ending June 6, 1917 only six such weapons were reported missing, all of which were on board planes shot down behind the German lines. None of them had been lost from 60 Squadron. It was strange, Greenhous added, that no one else reported noticing that the

Lewis gun was missing from Billy's plane.

Some have argued that Bishop must have landed somewhere, because he didn't have enough fuel to be away for as long as he was. But, in fact, he did. The Nieuport had an endurance of 2 hours 24 minutes, and Bishop was gone for only 1 hour 43 minutes.

As for the damage to Bishop's Nieuport, no one else reported seeing powder burns around the holes near the tail. Had the burns been there, it's hard to believe that they would have escaped the attention of the crowd of pilots and ground crews that quickly gathered to inspect the plane. Chief mechanic A. A. Nicod, who must be considered an expert witness when it came to aircraft battle damage, definitely believed Bishop, describing the raid as a "stupendous feat." In 1935 he wrote: "His machine was badly damaged by anti-aircraft fire and machine gun fire. There were a dozen bullet holes in the radius of a few inches just behind his head as he sat in the cockpit."

This evidence is crucial because it proves that Bishop was over enemy territory that morning. It's possible he could have shot bullet holes in his own plane with his own gun, but he obviously could not have brought along the flak cannons that would have been needed to inflict shrapnel damage.

Pilot William Molesworth of 60 Squadron made it clear, in a letter he wrote home that night, that he believed Bishop's story. And Jack Scott wrote at the bottom of the Canadian's combat report: "His machine is full of holes caused by machine gun fire from the ground." A squadron report that was sent on to authorities who were considering awarding Bishop the Victoria Cross for this exploit listed the damage as "17 bullet holes. Trailing edge of lower plane (wing) shot away in two bays." That document would appear to confirm that there were five bullet holes in the tail, as Fry recalled, a dozen in the fuselage just behind the cockpit, as Nicod had said, and shrapnel tears in the lower wing, as Nicod had also claimed.

But whatever Fry saw, or thought he saw, his testimony was not the only factor hurting Bishop's credibility. Somehow, a completely false rumour started to make the rounds about how many kills Billy was claiming to have made that day. According to one tale, the Canadian was insisting he had shot down no less than eight planes during the raid!

Pilot Frederick Libby, who was serving with 11 Squadron, wrote in his diary: "We have one pilot in our wing who writes a wicked report. He must be good but not quite as good as his last report. It seems early in the morning, before anyone else is up, he has his plane wheeled out, goes over a German airfield and routs the Huns out of their beds, strafes the hangars and waits for Mr. Hun to come up. The first two off the ground he knocks off, then gets two more trying to get off. The next two he chases into a tree and leaves them there like Santa Claus, then destroys two more, so home to breakfast. Anyway this guy isn't an Englishman. An Englishman would never write this kind of nonsense. God Almighty! Excuse me while I vomit."

Other pilots, he added, never made claims for victories that could not be confirmed.

Two Witnesses Uncovered

Indeed, the accusation that Bishop had no Allied witnesses for this raid — which won him the Victoria Cross — has been trotted out every time this controversial episode is discussed. But there *were* witnesses. Two people insisted they saw the raid.

The first was British balloonist Louis Weirter. Weirter's testimony was rejected for decades by many writers, because it was thought he was not close enough to have witnessed the attack. This author, for one, did not bother to include it in a biography he wrote about Bishop in 1988 because the story did not ring true at the time.

But new research shows that Weirter could easily have seen the carnage. Writing in the *Canadian Military Journal* in 2002, historian David Bashow noted that the local weather was quite good that morning, and the visibility looking down from above was particularly good. He added: "With the action occurring at Esnes and westward, Weirter would have been closer than previously thought, at approximately 10 miles range. On a clear day, a combat balloonist tethered at 4,000 feet could see as far as 40 miles, and had a formidable array of optical equipment to enhance his vision."

Bishop's critics have claimed that Weirter did not tell the authorities about the raid right away — he only came forward four months later when he was trying to sell a painting of the incident to a British museum. But no one can be sure what he said to his superiors, because most of the paperwork concerning Bishop's Victoria Cross has been lost, either destroyed by German bombers in the Second World War or culled by bureaucrats anxious to make space for new documents. All we know for certain is that a British serviceman in a position to see what was going on claimed to have witnessed the raid. It's entirely possible, perhaps even likely, that the authorities had a report from Weirter in their possession before deciding to grant Billy the VC.

The second witness was an old French farmer named Gaston Meuniers. Bashow revealed crucial new evidence collected by Canadian Group Captain Arnie Bauer during a 1984 interview with Meuniers. Meuniers, who was a 12-year-old boy living on a farm adjacent to Esnes airfield on June 2, 1917, claimed to have seen the attack. Speaking through an interpreter, the 81-year-old described the incident to Bauer in detail.

After talking with Bauer in 2002, Bashow wrote:

> *Specifically, Gaston Meuniers recalled hearing the Nieuport fire, presumably at ground targets, and he noted the British tricolour roundels on a Nieuport as it passed his vantage point. Shortly thereafter, he recalled seeing two aircraft shot down; one within the aerodrome boundary and another just outside of it.*

The boy was so proud of having witnessed the event that, after he read an article about it in the October 1917 issue of the French magazine *La Guerre Aerienne Ilustré*, he kept the publication for the rest of his life.

Meuniers' was not the only evidence that French civilians had seen Bishop's handiwork. Two German airfields were located in the area over which Bishop was flying, including a permanent facility at Estourmel and a temporary field a scant four miles away at Esnes. In between lay nothing but flat countryside, giving farmers working in nearby fields ringside seats to the fight. They not only saw what happened, they remembered it very clearly and told their story to a group of British pilots from 12 Squadron in the autumn of 1918. One of those fliers was Lieutenant Phil B. Townsend.

In a letter to a British aviation magazine in 1985, he wrote: "When we moved from Vaux Vrancourt (Somme) to the ex-German aerodrome at Estourmel, we were told that a British scout had attacked the German aircraft one morning in 1917 and had shot down three Huns."

When contacted by this author in 1986, Townsend said that he had learned this information from local French people. Two years later, Townsend qualified this statement, saying he hadn't talked directly to the civilians. His squadron mates had talked to them and relayed the news to him, he said. Still, as historian David Bashow points out, Townsend's testimony is interesting, "since it appears that farmers near Estourmel were aware of an attack somewhere in the vicinity at the appropriate time."

As for the French civilians telling 12 Squadron that the raid had occurred at Estourmel, Bashow speculated that they were referring to the Estourmel area, not the exact airfield location. He believes the aerodrome that Bishop attacked that morning was located at Esnes. With two landing strips so close together, that was certainly possible.

And there's even more evidence supporting Bishop's account. In 1962, American aviation writer Arch Whitehouse quoted German authorities as admitting that Bishop had attacked one of their aerodromes. However, they insisted he only made one quick firing pass, running for home as soon as the Albatroses took off to intercept him. In a 1981 interview, former Canadian cavalryman George Stirrett said that he had been with a group of Allied soldiers who took the crew of a German two-seater prisoner. The observer, he said, claimed that the airfield attack had been the talk of the entire German flying service.

The first *solid* confirmation from the German side was provided in 1993 by former Rumpler two-seater pilot Otto Roosen. Roosen, who was 97 years old at the time, told this author that he knew all about the raid. Asked specifically if he had learned about it during the war, he said, "Oh yes, we all knew about it. Our pilots talked about it for weeks. I talked to pilots who were there, but I can no longer remember their names."

So why don't German records show the losses? Probably

because none of the three pilots were killed or wounded by Bishop's fire. Surviving German records often only list airmen killed or wounded, making no mention of losses in which the crew walked away unhurt. Perhaps the planes the Canadian attacked that morning were not even badly damaged. Bishop's combat report states that the first two Albatroses were hit while flying extremely low to the ground. They were travelling slowly — just beginning to pick up speed as they lifted off the runway — when he pounced upon them.

The third claim presents more of a problem for Bishop's defenders because he said the aircraft crashed from 1,000 feet. At that height, a fatality, or at least a serious injury, was almost a certainty. But maybe the German pilot pulled up at the last second and made an emergency landing. Perhaps the line in Bishop's combat report claiming that the plane had hit the ground was simply autosuggestion. He may have assumed it *had* to have crashed, so why not just say that it did? That would explain why Gaston Meuniers could recall seeing only two German planes shot down that morning.

As with so many "victories" credited to Allied pilots during the Great War, these may not have been decisive kills. It's entirely possible that Bishop only damaged two planes and forced a third to land. Still, it could be argued that any pilot who had the courage to fly far behind enemy lines to attack an entire squadron by himself deserved the Victoria Cross, regardless of how much damage he may have caused.

Chapter Six
Ace of Aces

Bishop's ambition to become the war's greatest ace only intensified after his solo airfield raid. In letters home he kept comparing his victory score to that of other pilots, both Allied and German. "My total is now 36," he wrote in a letter to Margaret that summer, "making me second to Guynemer, the Frenchman, and third to Richthofen, the German, and second in record to any Englishman, Ball having 43."

He flew whenever the weather permitted, adding another 22 victories to his score between June 8 and August 16. And he achieved most of these while operating by himself. Flying deep behind enemy lines he would gain altitude, then come screaming down out of the sun on top of unsuspecting flights of German aircraft, or pilots shuttling from one point to another, convinced they were too far behind the trenches to be in any danger.

When attacking formations, Bishop would make his kill and get away in the confusion, before the survivors could regroup. His escapes were helped by his souped-up fighter, which had a much more powerful motor than other Nieuport 17s. Jack Scott had seen to that, securing for Bishop a 120-horsepower LeRhone engine that allowed him to sail along at about 112 miles per hour. The rest of 60 Squadron was making do with the standard 110-horsepower LeRhone that could only carry a Nieuport pilot forward at about 101 miles per hour. The difference may not seem like a lot today, but it could mean the difference between life and death in 1917.

Major Scott helped Billy to increase his score in other ways too, continuing to grant him victory credits in cases where he had no witnesses. The Englishman had his reasons for doing this. He knew that Bishop, with a roving commission, was free to fly 40 or more miles behind enemy lines. He often covered four times as much territory as the other pilots, who flew together on escort duty or offensive patrol near the front lines. Billy's chances of finding — and surprising — a German were much better than those of his comrades.

Scott also realized that Bishop was not an especially good team man. Once, when given charge of a newcomer called R. B. Clark, the Canadian led the rookie over the lines before taking off on his own in search of a victory. Clark, who was virtually helpless by himself, was jumped by three German fighters and shot down in flames. On another occasion, 60 Squadron pilot Sydney Pope recalled with annoyance how Bishop had left him in the lurch to go off on some private foray. Pope was taking photographs while Bishop provided overhead escort. They were operating deep behind enemy lines when Pope looked up for a moment and, to his astonishment, found himself absolutely alone and extremely vulnerable.

There can be little doubt that Bishop's bloodthirsty streak, his naked ambition and the favouritism that Scott showed him rankled some of 60 Squadron's other airmen. Willie Fry, for one, suspected that Bishop was padding his score with completely false claims. When he made that accusation to the Canadian's face, Scott insisted that Fry apologize. He flatly refused to do so and was sent home.

This isn't to say that Bishop was universally unpopular with his fellow airmen. Far from it. In his book *The History of 60 Squadron,* Jack Scott noted: "It was curious to notice how quick the mechanics of the squadron were to recognize Bishop's quality. Only a few days after his arrival at the squadron the sergeants gave a musical evening to which the officers were invited, and it was observed that one of the very few toasts which were proposed by them was to Bishop's health."

He was well liked by most pilots too. Billy was the unit's clown prince, and he kept everyone's morale up with a whole series of practical jokes. The writings and post-war recollections of several 60 Squadron pilots paint a picture of a happy-go-lucky individual who took the lead in off-duty social activities. Photos from the era show Bishop and his buddies locked arm-in-arm, laughing and obviously enjoying one another's company. However, as more and more of Bishop's friends were killed in action, he withdrew into himself. Over time, the exuberant extrovert became a charming but some-what distant character.

Of course, not all of Billy's victories during this period were scored on lone-wolf patrols. When he shot down a German fighter over Vitry on July 12, for example, the conquest was witnessed by famed Sopwith Triplane ace Robert Little and Nieuport pilot A. W. M. Mowle. One of two victories Billy claimed five days later was also solidly verified. He got in two bursts from point-blank range at an Albatros that was harassing a pair of Bristol two-seaters from 11 Squadron. Lieutenant Barnett, a gunner aboard one of the Bristols, saw the German plane go down in flames, minus part of its tail, a fact that was confirmed by 60 Squadron historian Joe Warne in a 1980 article he wrote for a British aviation magazine. And on August 5, while flying the new SE5 fighter, Bishop scored one his most spectacular victories of the war, leading William Molesworth and Spencer Horn into a bold attack on seven Albatroses.

In a letter home that night, Molesworth described what happened: "Our numbers were not overwhelming this time, but we knew the Huns had got pukka wind up by the way that they disappeared when we arrived on the line, so we felt quite confident in taking on twice as many as ourselves. Of course we were all out for trouble, as we wanted to show what the new machines could do. As soon as our leader [Bishop] spotted a formation of Huns, he was after them like a flash. I think there were seven of them but we were all much too excited to count. Suddenly they saw us coming and tried desperately to escape, but our leader got into his favourite position, and the rear Hun hadn't a ghost of a chance. The next instant he was a flaming mass."

The next day, Bishop tied Albert Ball's record, shooting down an Albatros in front of the Bristol two-seater crew of Captain "Steve" Clement and Lieutenant Ralph Carter from 22 Squadron. Neither man is listed in RFC records as a witness, but Carter wrote in his diary that night: "We heard 'archie' [anti-aircraft fire] over here today so 'Steve' and I went up. We ran into five EA scouts and fought with them from 3 p.m. till 4:15 p.m. Bishop on an SE5 joined us and he sent one down."

Three days later, Bishop downed an Aviatik two-seater, making him the top scoring ace — living or dead — of the entire Royal Flying Corps.

Combat Fatigue

All of this frenzied activity came at a price. In a letter home around this time, Bishop admitted that his nerves were shaky and added, "I find myself shuddering at chances I didn't think of taking six weeks ago." Clearly, he was suffering from combat fatigue.

More than that, he was beginning to feel guilty about having slain so many men. After a friend was killed in action, Billy wrote a revealing letter to Margaret: "I am thoroughly downcast tonight. The Huns got Lloyd today, such a fine fellow too, and one of our best pilots. Sometimes all of this awful fighting in the air makes you wonder if you have a right to call yourself human. My honey, I am so sick of it all, the killing, the war. All I want is home and you."

Here was a new Bishop. The correspondence contained none of the bitter vows of vengeance that had marked his earlier comments after other friends had been killed. Eventually, he would become sick to death of the violence. He made that clear during a visit to the Seventh Canadian Mounted Rifles, who occasionally found themselves stationed near Filescamp Farm. Bishop told his old friend George Stirrett about the time he'd shot a German pilot down from close range. "My bullets shattered his face and skull. I can't get that picture out of my mind," he said.

Perhaps he was thinking of that particular kill when he wrote in his 1918 autobiography: "Once or twice the idea that a live man had been piloting the machine would occur and recur to me, and it would worry me a bit. My sleep would be spoiled for perhaps a night. I did not relish the idea even of killing Germans." This was an astonishing public admission that somehow got past the wartime censors.

Billy found a much-needed tonic from the war in the city of Amiens, where he met a beautiful young French girl named Ninette. In her company he found a gentle woman who seemed to understand his needs. She placed no demands on him and never expressed the slightest concern for his safety. That in turn made it easier for him to relax and forget the war for a few hours at a time. During the bitter days ahead, Ninette would help Bishop through some very traumatic times. And although he had by no means forgotten about Margaret, without Ninette as his mistress during this stressful period, he probably would not have survived.

Returning to action, Bishop claimed two victories during a solo flight on August 13. He was flying above the clouds when he realized he had been spotted by three enemy aircraft, slightly above him. Their leader outdistanced the other two and attacked, so Bishop turned his aircraft and approached him head-on.

In his combat report he described the action: "At 300 yards I opened fire and he immediately swerved. I continued firing and passed quite close to him. On looking over my shoulder I saw him burst into flames and dive. One of the others then attacked, the third one shooting from 500 yards at the same time at me. I maneuvered with the second one and fired a burst, then managed to get on his tail. At 50 yards I opened fire. He burst into flames after about 20 rounds and fell in a spin." As the two enemy aircraft fell ablaze, Bishop dived through the clouds after the third, but he was too far away and escaped.

Two days later he claimed a two-seater down out of control for his 48th victory. Then, on the evening of August 16, he recorded two more triumphs. Flying alone once again, he snuck up on a two-seater, shooting its wings off. Two Albatroses approached, then thought better of it and turned for home. As they retreated, Bishop fired a burst from long range, hitting one of them. "He went into a spin and I watched him crash half a mile north of Carvin," he wrote in his combat report. "The other enemy aircraft escaped."

With that, Bishop flew home and packed his bags. He had been promoted to the rank of major, awarded a second Distinguished Service Order and ordered to report to Buckingham Palace, where he would receive his Victoria Cross from the king. From there he was headed to Canada, where the authorities planned to use him to sell an increasingly unpopular war to the public.

Above left: Bishop as a schoolboy in cadet school.
Above right: Billy Bishop as a gunner/observer with 21
Squadron in 1916.
Bottom: Billy Bishop with his girlfriend.

Top: Bishop about to take off on a mission. He sometimes flew without helmet and goggles, claiming that he enjoyed the wind in his hair.

Left: An Albatros that crashed without bursting into flames. In cases in which the pilot survived — as may well have happened here — German records would not mention the loss of the plane.

Right: Bishop in full flying gear in front of 60 Squadron headquarters. In the doorway from left to right, Lieutenant H. W. Guy and Major Scott.

Top: Bishop and Margaret are married in 1917.
Bottom: In front of his famed Nieuport 17. Bishop claimed nearly forty victories with this machine before switching to the faster SE5.

Left: An official photo of Bishop widely distributed during the war for propaganda purposes.

Below: Bishop (left) with William Molesworth and Graham Young outside 60 Squadron's "Saloon Bar."

Bottom: A German aircraft of Jasta 12 lined up. Bishop claimed victories over two of these aircraft on Aug. 5, 1917.

Top left: A downed German plane.
Top right: Manfred von Richtofen, the "Red Baron," flying ace of WWI.
Bottom: Paul Billik, the high-scoring German ace who was lightly wounded by Bishop, stands beside his swastika-decorated Albatros.

Top: Bishop relaxes between missions.
Right: Bishop (left) with Major Jack Scott.

Top: Bishop (left) and Lieutenant-Colonel William Barker
pose with a captured German Fokker.
Bottom: The house where Bishop grew up.

Above: Bishop as an Air Marshal in 1944.

Chapter Seven
Propaganda Symbol

Billy Bishop arrived back in Canada in the fall of 1917 to find himself on display — much like a prize steer at a country fair — in the expectation that his appearance would rekindle public enthusiasm for a war that had lost its glamour. The federal government had gone so far as to commission a marble bust of the war hero.

By late 1917, the conflict was tearing Canada apart. Casualties were now reaching catastrophic proportions. The Canadian army, which had won undeniably spectacular victories, was badly depleted and there were not enough volunteers coming forward to fill the gaps created by German machine guns. The situation was so serious that the House of Commons had passed a conscription act, the Military Service Act, in July.

The draft created bitter divisions in the country, splitting the population along linguistic lines. In Quebec, French Canadians viewed the war as simply another of Europe's endless conflicts and angrily opposed conscription. There was talk of separation for the first time. Farmers across the country were upset as well, because they needed their sons to help them in the fields. When Ottawa introduced an income tax for the first time in history, saying that it was needed to pay for the war, there was still more acrimony.

Bishop was a godsend to the authorities, who were quick to realize that the swaggering fighter pilots in their leather helmets, silk scarves and goggles had captured the imagination of millions of ordinary people. In Britain, a Member of Parliament referred to them as "Knights of the Air" and the slogan had caught on.

Most Canadians had never even seen a flying machine — the airplane had only been invented 11 years before the war began — let alone flown in one. Now they were reading death-defying tales of gallant young men jousting with one another high above the clouds in their little wood-and-fabric, open-cockpit biplanes. These men flew without parachutes, armour plating, radar or even radios. If a single bullet hit the gas tank, they would plunge to the earth enveloped in flames. Their victory "scores" were tabulated and fed to a public that gobbled them up in much the same way that today's sports fans check the newspapers to find out who is leading in the National Hockey League.

The fact that Bishop was young, handsome and charming made him all the more appealing. He was sent around the country giving speeches to enormous crowds. In Toronto, a mob broke through barriers to get at him, and he rode down Bay Street in a parade. In Massey Hall, a standing-room-only crowd shouted itself hoarse when he showed up to give a talk about his adventures.

The authorities would not tolerate anyone who might lessen his impact, as is made clear by a short item that appeared in the October 24, 1917 edition of the British magazine *The Aeroplane*. Bishop had demonstrated his expertise by flying an instruction plane at Leaside Camp on October 18 in front of an admiring crowd. "A young cadet in another machine proceeded to imitate his feats and accomplished everything that Major Bishop had done," read the news report "The cadet was placed under close arrest for deviating from the instructions given him before he ascended."

The press coverage was fawning on both sides of the Atlantic, with reporters in Canada, the United States and England painting a picture of a modest hero. A Toronto *Globe* journalist who watched Bishop address an adoring crowd got caught up in the excitement. He wrote: "If I am any judge of expressions I should say that Bishop would rather be most anywhere else than where he was at that moment. He was more rattled at meeting that enthusiastic, admiring crowd than he would have been suddenly meeting an enemy aviator while turning a corner among the clouds. Though I had seen many receptions of this kind I admit that this was the first one that gave me a real thrill and I cheered for all I was worth."

In Owen Sound, the *Sun* was even more gushing: "He had been received by the king at Buckingham Palace, he had been feted in England and ever since his return to Canada, but he is still the same modest Billy Bishop that the English papers call him," it reported. In the United Kingdom, a publication called the *Weekly Dispatch* described Bishop as "a slight, fair-haired youth, with a pleasant face." It also emphasized his modesty. "Canada's famous 19-year-old [sic] airman has returned to his native land," it reported on September 30, 1917. "On his arrival he was asked to narrate some of his more extraordinary experiences. 'I haven't had any,' he said!"

The newspaper admitted that Bishop's story was being reported to help boost public morale. "With its proverbial modesty the Royal Flying Corps was loath to publish the deeds of any particular airman, but with the Germans continually boasting of their crack fighting pilots it was felt imperative that we too should publish the deeds of our champion pilots," it said.

In the United States there was an equally favourable reaction. After Bishop addressed a crowd of 800 at the Biltmore Hotel in New York City, a reporter described him as "a mere slip of a boy, looking not at all his twenty-three years and weighing not much more than 100 pounds." He added, "Looking like a college freshman, he told of his exploits in a manner as cool as if he were reciting a lesson in a classroom."

Marriage

For a time, Bishop was here, there and everywhere. One day he was in London, Ontario, visiting sick children in hospital, the next he was in Dayton, Ohio, meeting with Orville Wright, one of the inventors of the airplane.

Through it all, he found the time to make wedding plans. In fact, Margaret had been at the dockside in Montreal when he disembarked from the ship that brought him from England. After an ecstatic reunion, the couple decided to get married, setting October 17 as the wedding date. His future father-in-law still had his reservations, but he could hardly object to his daughter marrying Canada's most famous war hero.

Given Billy's antics with Ninette in France, his decision to get married may seem surprising. But Margaret was the woman he loved, and there had never been any doubt between them that one day they would be husband and wife. The wedding, which was held at Toronto's Timothy Eaton Church, was a fairy-tale affair of a kind not seen before in Canada. The handsome young warrior marrying his beautiful childhood sweetheart — it was a made-to-order romance that took the public's mind off more pressing matters. As Billy and Margaret left the church, they passed under an arch of ceremonial swords drawn by Canadian cavalry officers. Throngs of spectators followed the newlyweds to the Burden home and, later, to the train station as they left for their honeymoon in New York's Catskill Mountains.

Even on his honeymoon, Billy couldn't escape from the war completely. He began work on his autobiography, which was completed in a few months and quickly became a best seller.

Finally, in January 1918, his leave was over and a well-rested Bishop was sent to England to organize his own fighter squadron, No. 85, which he promptly nicknamed "The Flying Foxes." Although he had enjoyed the attention he received in Canada, he was anxious to get back into action. His revulsion at the thought of killing had been replaced by a burning desire to reclaim his title as the top gun of the Allied flying services. During Bishop's leave, Englishman Jimmy McCudden had scored an astounding 49 victories, bringing his total up to 57.

Bishop had been dethroned as the British Empire's ace of aces and he didn't like it one bit. The Red Baron, meanwhile, had brought his score up to 80 victories. If Billy was going to become the war's highest scoring ace, he had a lot of ground to make up. But before he could return to the front, the high command insisted he take a brief refresher course. After becoming familiar with the new, twin-gun SE5a, a fast, sturdy biplane that could fly at 122 miles per hour and climb to 22,000 feet, he was allowed to pick his own men for his squadron.

Bishop took the unusual step of organizing his group on the basis of personality. According to pilot Larry Callahan: "He went to barrooms in London and finally showed up with an assortment that were highly congenial and had been through many tests and could be depended on to stand by under trouble."

One of those he selected was Elliott White Springs, a

South Carolina native destined to become one of the leading American aces of the war. He had no illusions, however, that Bishop had selected him for his flying abilities, admitting that Billy had chosen him because of his bartending skills! There may have been some truth in that, because Springs was a party animal who kept spirits high.

As fellow 85 Squadron pilot Mac Grider wrote in his diary, "I don't think Bishop is sorry he brought us along. We are the only outfit at the front that has ice cream for dinner every night. Springs has taught the cook to make Eggs Benedict and we breakfast well. In fact, although 'in the midst of life we are in death' we manage to have a lot of fun — chicken livers en brochette, champagne and Napoleon brandy. We decided it was too much trouble to sign chits for drinks in the mess. So all drinks are to be free and each man will have to see that he gets his money's worth."

With his team in place, Bishop led his squadron across the channel, arriving at Petit Synthe airfield, just outside Dunkirk, on May 22, 1918. His final tour of duty was about to begin.

Chapter Eight
Last Hurrah

I t didn't take Bishop long to make his mark once he returned to the Western Front. Flying alone on May 27, 1918 he snuck up on a German two-seater and shot it down.

Over the next four days he added six more victories, to surpass McCudden's record. All seven of these kills were scored on lone-wolf patrols. But although there were no aerial witnesses, Bishop's combat reports have a ring of truth, as was demonstrated on May 31, when he took part in three fights. In his first report for the day he says: "I attacked one of three Pfalz scouts sitting 2,000 feet above a formation of about fourteen enemy aircraft. I fired 20 rounds at 20 yards range from behind. Enemy aircraft immediately fell completely out of control. I was unable to watch it owing to presence of the remainder of the enemy aircraft formation." There is no claim that the German aircraft broke up in the air, went down in flames, or even crashed.

His second report is equally modest. It reads: "I attacked a two-seater enemy aircraft who was evidently an artillery observation machine. I fired a long burst from rear at 100 yards range, enemy aircraft turned to left, then dived east and landed in a field." Again, there was no claim of destruction.

Five hours later, he filled out his third combat report for the day: "Seeing white Archies [anti-aircraft fire] two miles east of Hazebrook I flew in that direction and saw one enemy aircraft scout underneath me near the A.A. burst. I dived at him but suddenly saw another enemy aircraft higher just re-crossing the enemy lines, followed him and fired 20 rounds from each gun at 50 yards range. Enemy aircraft fell to bits and fell two miles north of Estaires. This enemy aircraft must have been seen by A.A. batteries of the 2nd Army as visibility was very good."

Indeed it was. Mac Grider wrote in his diary that night: "They are changing the score now as the major has just come down and has shot down two more Huns — a scout and a two-seater. Archie [the crew of an Allied anti-aircraft battery] saw one of them go down and another one broke-up in the air."

When June arrived there were witnesses to Bishop's exploits because he was now leading his pilots on missions across the lines. On June 1 he reported: "While on practice patrol, I led patrol consisting of Captain Horn, Lieut. MacGregor, Lieut. Springs, diving on six enemy aircraft. I fired four bursts at one enemy aircraft, zoomed and dived again onto the leader's tail, fired 30 rounds from 50 yards, enemy aircraft went down in a straight dive, then spun and crashed near La Gorgue. Lieut. Springs confirms the enemy aircraft I shot down."

The next day his combat report told of an even more audacious attack: "I led Lieut. Callahan and Lieut. Thomson diving on eight E.A [enemy aircraft]. I fired at four different E. A., one of which fell out of control for 1,500 feet, then broke up in pieces. This machine was seen and confirmed falling out of control by Lieut. Callahan."

In just three days Bishop had scored three witnessed victories. He had also shown exceptional daring in full view of other Allied servicemen. Had these three battles been the only dogfights of his career, they would have been more than enough to earn him his status as a hero.

When he wasn't certain that his opponent had been destroyed, Bishop was honest enough to say so. On June 4, 1918, for example, he was credited with two victories, even though he made it clear in his combat report that he did not see one of his adversaries crash. It reads: "Seeing a formation of eight enemy aircraft out to sea, I flew towards them from the east and diving, attacked a straggler, after 10 rounds from each gun, he burst into flames and fell burning brightly. I zoomed away and escaped." Then, nine minutes later he attacked another straggler from the same formation. "Diving from the east on them and zooming away, fired 30 rounds from each gun at 75 yards range," he reported. "Enemy aircraft, which was a silver Albatros, fell completely out of control and passed through clouds 8,000 feet below still out of control." In this particular instance Bishop was credited with one *destroyed* and one *down out of control* victory.

All this success had the squadron in a euphoric mood. And in the same way that Bishop had become addicted to combat in 1917, so now did some of the pilots under his command. Mac Grider, writing to his sister after his first dogfight, said, "God, it was Great! Sherman was all wrong. He was unlucky enough to be in the wrong branch of the service. We have nineteen Huns to our credit and nobody missing. It's as safe as a church if you know the game, and I am learning under past masters so don't be too uneasy about me."

He credited the squadron's success at least partly to Bishop's informal leadership. "This is surely a wonderful bunch," he wrote. "I would like you to know them. They worry about nothing at all and our nights are a series of song and good cheer. We have a piano and a victrola. It is a big family, there is no discipline. We have breakfast from eight to eleven and everyone is happy. Everybody is keen on the job; you are not afraid of being let down in a scrap."

But they were playing a very dangerous game, as became evident a few days later, when Lobo Benbow was shot down just inside his own lines. He was the first 85 Squadron man to die in action and Bishop would not allow his pilots to attend the funeral, fearing it would be too upsetting for them. Not long after that, Grider himself was killed.

Final Victories

In the middle of June the squadron moved to a tiny airfield

near the village of St. Omer. "We are on a beautiful, wooded hill overlooking the field and there's a pretty sylvan glade on the other side where we can snooze in the breeze," Elliott White Springs wrote in a letter home. Bishop added to the pleasant atmosphere by picking up several stray dogs, along with a cow and a goat. But he had not lost his skills in combat, claiming two victories on June 16 and three more the next day. One of his victims on the 17th may have been Rumpler two-seater pilot Otto Roosen, who came down behind his own lines with a dead observer in the rear cockpit.

Roosen, who moved to Canada after the Second World War, told a number of aviation historians that Bishop had shot him down that morning. When this author tracked him down at his Bracebridge, Ontario home in 1993, the 97-year-old repeated the same story.

"I was flying a Rumpler and Billy Bishop came from the sun," he recalled. "He caught me by surprise and it was all over very quickly. He shot me down from behind and shot my navigator dead. The engine stopped and I had to land in a field on my side of the lines."

As impressive as these performances may have been, they paled in comparison to what Bishop was about to claim. He scored two victories on June 18 to raise his score to an even 70 (counting his three balloons). But when he landed that evening, he was told he was being posted back to England. The Canadian government, fearful that his death would be a serious blow to public morale, had asked that he be sent home. Undeterred, he took off alone the next morning and, flying in overcast conditions, claimed an incredible five victories.

"After crossing the lines in the clouds I came out over Ploegsteert Wood, saw three Pfalz scouts which I attacked," he said in his combat report. "Two other Pfalz then approached from the east." It was five against one, with three German fighters in front of him and two more closing in on his tail. Ignoring the enemy to his rear as best he could, Bishop went straight for the trio in front of him. A withering burst of fire sent one down in flames. The other two, swerving to avoid his tracers, came together in a sickening mid-air collision and plunged to the ground. Turning on the pair behind him, he caught one with a burst from 200 yards, sending it spinning into the mud. The fifth Pfalz escaped into the clouds, Bishop said.

Still not satisfied, he kept searching the sky for fresh victims. A few minutes later, he encountered a two-seater and reported shooting it down in flames. With no more enemy machines to be found, Bishop strafed a small body of soldiers with a prolonged burst of fire. Then, out of ammunition and low on fuel, he flew home.

Not everyone believed this story. Pilot Ira Jones of 74 Squadron was fairly dripping with sarcasm when he called it "Bishop's wonderful feat." But at 85 Squadron, the pilots who had seen Bishop in action from time to time harboured no doubts. Springs commented, "pretty good morning. That's something for the boys to shoot at. He's made something of this squadron, too." That afternoon, the whole squadron flew with Billy as far as Boulogne, where they broke out the champagne to toast him. Then they gathered on the tarmac to watch his SE5a lift off and fly back to England.

"So our major is gone," Springs wrote that night. "But if ever a C.O. had the respect, admiration and love of his unit 'twas him. The mechanics even are disconsolate."

Chapter Nine
Adjusting to the Peace

When the First World War ended on November 11, 1918, Bishop had a difficult time adjusting to the peace. He travelled across North America for a time, giving lectures to sellout crowds for huge sums of money. But before long, the adoring throngs disappeared. The world was tired of war and war heroes. During one engagement, just 10 people turned out to hear him talk. Disappointed, he cancelled the rest of the tour.

He lived off his wife's income for a time and then went into business with fellow Canadian ace William Barker. The two Victoria Cross winners set up their own airline, selling shares to prominent businessmen in Toronto and Montreal in order to raise enough cash to buy three war-surplus seaplanes. Although the machines were only designed to hold three passengers, Bishop transported five each time he flew. He took them from Toronto harbour to Muskoka cottage country and, except for a few months in the summer, there wasn't enough business to keep them in the black. Inevitably, the business went bankrupt.

Billy next tried his hand at stunt flying, buying an old biplane and performing aerobatics at the Canadian National Exhibition. On one occasion he dived recklessly toward the grandstand, terrifying thousands of spectators, who stampeded out of their seats in a state of panic. One woman claimed she had a miscarriage. That was the end of his career as a showman.

Billy and Margaret spent the next 10 years in England. She raised their two children and he made a fortune working as a salesman for a company that manufactured iron pipe. But he lost it all in the stock market crash of 1929. Returning to Canada, he accepted a position with an oil company in Montreal and was soon on his feet again.

When the Second World War broke out in 1939, Bishop was rushed back into uniform, this time as a figurehead with the rank of air marshal. Placed in charge of recruitment, he proved to be a tireless worker. During a trip to the still-neutral United States, he set up a program that lured hundreds of American volunteers to the Royal Canadian Air Force. Before long, he was one of the key people behind the establishment of the British Commonwealth Training Plan, which trained 167,000 Allied airmen in Canada.

He stumped the country, giving speeches from Halifax to Victoria. Young people were deeply impressed with his record and they flocked to RCAF recruiting stations after each of his appearances. While the army and navy had trouble finding enough men to meet their needs, the airforce found itself turning people away. Bishop also helped sell war bonds and served as an inspirational figure to those who had already signed up, pinning wings on new pilots and conducting endless inspection tours.

In many ways, Bishop's recruitment effort was his finest hour. His exploits in the First World War had demanded great courage, but the conflict itself was seen by many as a needless exercise that could easily have been avoided, had a handful of men of vision been in the halls of power in 1914. The Second World War was different. History shows that it was not possible to negotiate with the Nazis. The world had to stand up to them or be enslaved. Bishop, by helping to make the RCAF one of the most powerful airforces on the planet, played an honourable role in their defeat.

After the war, Bishop went into semi-retirement, spending his time reading and occupying his time with various hobbies. But in the last dozen years of his life a dramatic change took place — Billy Bishop became a passionate anti-war crusader.

Epilogue

Bishop's conversion to a campaigner for peace is an aspect of his life that is almost unknown today, even among those who think they know his story well. Yet, as we have seen, his revulsion for the whole grisly business of war began to surface in the middle of his first tour of duty as a fighter pilot, when a buddy was killed in action.

The cold-hearted warrior, who had hated his enemies with all his heart, would soon mellow even further. Not long after the Great War ended, Bishop was expressing generous praise for his former adversaries. As early as January 1919, the San Antonio *Light* reported his admiration for the sportsmanlike qualities of two well-known German aces, Captains Boelcke and Immelmann. According to the newspaper, Bishop said: "They were both very, very fine fliers, and were regarded by our boys as very alert and ingenious, and capable of making the most of any situation."

Even the Red Baron, who had been killed in action on April 21, 1918, came in for praise from the Canadian. In a magazine article written in the 1930s, Bishop had this to say about his one-time bitter rival: "The burial of Richthofen behind the British lines was a just and fitting tribute to the wonderful career of that great German soldier. He was buried with the fullest of military honours, and not an aviator in the whole of our flying forces but felt but a real pang of sorrow that such a great career should be ended — although it goes without saying that the fact that he had been eliminated from the German forces was to us all a tremendous relief. However (although he probably would not have wished it himself), it would have been to us much more satisfactory if he could have been captured and his life spared."

While on a business trip to Berlin in 1928, Bishop made a private visit to Richthofen's grave. The world would never have known that he had paid his respects except for the fact that an alert cemetery groundskeeper recognized him and contacted the German Air Aces Association. This distinguished veterans' group tracked Bishop down and invited him to dinner. The Canadian veteran agreed to come. He even accepted an honourary membership from the organization! Commenting on this extraordinary event, the Ottawa *Citizen* said: "Colonel Bishop's breaking of bread with his old foes is an example to us all. It would be a great pity, and a great loss if this spirit were retarded by acts of Germany's conquerors. A far better and wiser course has been shown by Colonel Bishop."

Bishop corresponded with Hermann Goering, the much-decorated fighter pilot who had assumed command of the Richthofen's squadron after the Red Baron's death. Later, when Goering became Adolf Hitler's right-hand man, Bishop severed all ties with him. But he remained fond of Ernest Udet, the famed German ace with 62 Allied planes to his credit. Udet felt the same way about the Canadian, referring to Billy as "my friend and comrade Bishop, who is the greatest English scouting ace."

Eventually, Bishop became utterly disillusioned with combat. When interviewed about his wartime autobiography, he said, "It is so terrible that I cannot read it today. It turns my stomach. It was headline stuff, whoop-de-doo, red-hot, hurray for our side stuff."

During the Second World War, he was alarmed as he read stories of massed air attacks on the civilian populations of Europe. As the fighting was drawing to a close, he called on the world's leaders to knock down international boundaries and to ensure that the airplane would be used in future for trade, tourism and goodwill visits — not warfare. Few have any idea just how much of a peacenik he had become. In his largely ignored 1944 book, *Winged Peace*, he wrote: "We can no longer afford the bitter luxury of war. Civilian populations, women and children by the thousands, tens of thousands of old men and women in their declining years, were destroyed during the course of the Second World War.... In future wars civilian populations will be at the mercy of any aggressor, for aggression will come without warning and its impact will be so terrific that what has happened to Europe during World War II will be picayune by comparison."

It was crucial, he continued, to abandon the narrow pursuit of nationalism. In an even more forceful passage from the same book, he wrote: "If we take to the skies again to settle our disputes, such havoc will result that our civilization itself will collapse under the blow.... We have been confronted during this century by the most serious and urgent lessons ever to face the human species and we have been confronted by them not once but twice."

Bishop expressed the fear that most people were willing to accept once again the pre-war nationalistic and racial divisions that had brought about the war in the first place: "If we have not learned from World War II that we dare not fight again, because to fight will mean the annihilation of civilization itself, then what has capitalism on one hand or conglomerate socialism on the other to do with it?"

He wrote these comments a year before the Americans began dropping atomic bombs on Japanese cities, and 57 years before the terrorist attacks on New York and Washington. Bishop went further, expressing confidence that people could get along, if only they got to know one another, to appreciate each other's cultures, and to accept a kind of global citizenship. War could only be avoided in the future, he believed, if "we recognize and accept the implications of world citizenship, superimposed on national citizenship."

The airplane, he added, could help mankind secure world unity. "We can use the air for peace," he said. "Tomorrow I hope our young citizens, in hundreds and thousands, will fly from country to country and come to know each other, come to know the lore and traditions of each other's native lands, and, what is more important, enjoy the free exchange of ideas which is only possible when people can meet face to face, talk to each other and live together."

He ridiculed the isolationists in the United States who had blocked the formation of the League of Nations in 1919, and he endorsed the concept of the United Nations, which would became a reality four years after *Winged Peace* appeared.

Ten years before the arms race of the mid-1950s, he warned against such a possibility. Twenty years before the civil rights movement of the 1960s transformed the United States and 30 years before multiculturalism took hold in Canada, Bishop was calling for more understanding between the races. The establishment of a world culture, he said, was essential.

All of these opinions represent an astounding turnabout for Bishop. Like many Canadians born in the nineteenth century, he had exhibited racist traits from time to time. While serving at the Front in 1917 he had given his dog, a big black hound, the vile name "Nigger." In a 1918 letter to Margaret in which he bemoaned the death of a friend, he wrote, "Poor Lobo, he was a white man through and through and the Squadron loved him, as I did."

In 1927, he co-authored an adventure novel called *The Flying Squad* in which the villain, a character named Rosenbaum, is referred to frequently as "the Jew" or "the little Jew." One particularly offensive passage tells how the book's two heroes stumble upon Rosenbaum in the forest. It reads:

"The other was short and stout: his whole countenance proclaimed the Jew. He was clad in a dark gray suit more suitable to the main thoroughfares of a big city than to wandering in the woods." The same stereotypical theme is found elsewhere in the book.

Bishop's co-author, Major Rothesay Stuart-Wortley, may have been responsible for this shameful gibberish. It is possible that Bishop may only have lent his name to the book to help sell copies. But we must assume that he saw proofs of the novel before it went to press, then let it be published under his name. But 12 years later the apparently anti-Semitic Bishop was working tirelessly, putting his health at considerable risk, to help the Allies defeat the Nazis. And even before the world found out about the Holocaust, he was renouncing all forms of racism

***

As the end of his life approached, Bishop remembered his squadron mates with warmth, describing them as grand fellows. "I formed friendships which will never die. That is youth's genius in wars," he said, "and the only good that comes of them."

The end finally came for Billy Bishop on September 11, 1956. He died in his sleep, aged 62 years. Having seen so much insanity in his time, he had turned completely against war and hatred.

Appendix

Bishop's Victories

Billy Bishop was credited with 75 victories — 72 planes and three balloons.

Fifty-four of those airplanes are listed in official records as having been destroyed. But the actual number of enemy aircraft that he sent down was probably far fewer. A study of his combat reports shows that he claimed 24 opponents as driven down out of control, driven down or forced to land. In several cases Major Scott upgraded Bishop's more modest claims to the 'destroyed' classification. In other instances, Royal Flying Corps senior brass did the same thing after Scott had left Bishop's original claim unchanged. That's why, for example, his 'down out of control' claim of April 30, 1917, shows up in official records in the 'destroyed' category. It also explains why a similar claim on May 31, 1918, was later classified as destroyed.

Some historians have suggested that the authorities upgraded Bishop's claims to improve morale, and they're probably right. But that was hardly Bishop's fault. He was not the charlatan that some have suggested. Indeed, his combat reports were often very modest. Even in 1917, when Scott was confirming virtually everything that Bishop claimed, we find numerous statements indicating his uncertainty about whether or not he had hit his target or about its subsequent fate.

Then there is the matter of witnesses for Bishop's claims. In October 1984, Joe Warne, the official historian of 60 Squadron, sent this author a list of the ace's 1917 victories. It included 10 that he believed were "confirmed by witness" and eight others in which, he said, "I deduce that others confirmed the action because Bishop was flying as a member of a patrol." In those cases, however, he could find no specific record of witnesses. He came to his conclusions after poring over a huge collection of data.

I was able to find several witnesses whose accounts don't show up in the official records. Instead, I discovered them in logbooks, letters and diaries and during interviews I conducted with First World War veterans in the 1980s. One that comes immediately to mind was Bishop's claim for July 29, 1917. On that date Bishop and fellow 60 Squadron pilots Keith Caldwell and Bill Gunner became involved in a fight with four Albatroses over Vitry. Gunner was killed and Caldwell was forced to withdraw when his guns jammed, leaving Bishop alone. At that point, another three Germans joined in.

In his book, Brereton Greenhous listed this as an unwitnessed kill, saying that Bishop made his claim after Caldwell had left the scene.

But according to Bishop's autobiography, Caldwell

courageously came back into the fray without any working weapons, hoping to bluff the Germans into retreating. In a log entry written that night, Caldwell seems to confirm that account. He wrote: "With Gunner and Bishop. Attacked four EA [enemy aircraft] over Vitry. We drifted N. of Douai, three more EA came in. Both guns jammed; came home low escorted by two EA down to 80 feet."

Clearly, Caldwell knew that seven Germans were involved in the fight, not just the four who were there when he first pulled out. This would certainly suggest that he came back to assist Bishop. Besides, author David Baker, in his book *William Avery "Billy" Bishop: The Man and the Aircraft He Flew*, says that Bishop scored his kill before Caldwell left, when there were only four Germans present. Either way, it appears that Caldwell was on the scene and in a position to see Bishop score his victory, which is undoubtedly why Warne listed it as a triumph that he believed was witnessed.

It appears that Warne was right. Former 60 Squadron pilot Tim Hervey, who kept in contact with a number of his old comrades after the war, told this author that Caldwell had related the story of the jammed guns to him, confirming that he had indeed charged back into the fight, unable to shoot at his antagonists. Caldwell, Hervey added, told him that he had seen Bishop down one of the Germans. Critics may dismiss this as second-hand evidence, but I question whether oral history should be so easily discarded.

Warne's list did not include any of Bishop's three victories claimed on June 2 that won him the VC. But if we are to accept the accounts of Louis Weirter and Gaston Meuniers, we can add two or three witnessed kills to his 1917 total.

In 1918, meanwhile, five of his 25 claims were witnessed, according to a number of sources, including official records, letters and diaries of Bishop's squadron mates and oral history recounted to this author by First World War veterans during interviews in the 1980s.

And, of course, there may have been other witnesses that we don't know about. Tim Hervey told this author that Major Scott sometimes didn't bother to record in writing victory confirmations that were phoned in from other squadrons. "Nobody complained about it because the major was generous in granting victories," Hervey said.

Still, it's true that the majority of Bishop's victories were not witnessed by anyone on the Allied side. And German records do not prove much of anything because they are incomplete.

In the end, it's more accurate to say that Bishop won 75 fights than it is to say he scored that many 'kills.' Many of his triumphs were moral victories at best, with his opponents only being damaged or chased away. However, even Bishop's harshest critics have been quick to admit that he was a very brave man. And all but the most mean-spirited will concede he was a very high-scoring ace with an amazing record in battle.

Bibliography

Baker, David. *William Avery "Billy" Bishop: The Man and the Aircraft He Flew*. London: Outline Press, 1990.

Bashow, David. *Knights of the Air: Canadian Fighter Pilots in the First World War*. Toronto: McArthur and Co., 2000.

Bishop, Arthur. *The Courage of the Early Morning*. Toronto: McClelland and Stewart Ltd., 1965.

Bishop, William and Stuart-Wortley, Rothesay. *The Flying Squad*. New York: The Sun Dial Press, Inc., 1927.

Bishop, William. *Winged Warfare*. Toronto: A Totem Book, 1976.

Bishop, William. *Winged Peace*. Toronto: McMillan Company of Canada Ltd., 1944.

Davis, Burke. *War Bird: The Life and Times of Elliott White Springs*. Chapel Hill and London: The University of North Carolina Press, 1987.

Fry, William. *Air of Battle*. London: William-Kimber and Company, 1974.

Greenhous, Brereton. *The Making of Billy Bishop*. Toronto: The Dundurn Group, 2002.

Kilduff, Peter. *Red Baron: The Life and Death of an Ace*. Newton Abbot: David and Charles, 2007.

Jones, Ira. *Tiger Squadron*. London: W. H. Allen and Company, 1954.

Bibliography

Libby, Frederick. *Horses Don't Fly*. New York: Arcade
  Publishing, 2000.
Mathieson, W.D. *Billy Bishop, VC*. Markham: Fitzhenry
  and Whiteside Ltd., 1989.
McCaffery, Dan. *Billy Bishop: Canadian Hero*. Toronto:
  James Lorimer & Company Ltd., 2002.
Nowarra, H. J. and Kimbrough Brown. *Von Richthofen and
  the Flying Circus*. Los Angeles: Aero Publications, 1964.
Scott, Jack. *The History of 60 Squadron, RAF*. London:
  Heinemann Publishers, 1919.
Springs, Elliott White. *War Birds: The Diary of an
  Unknown Aviator*. London: Temple Press, 1966.

Other sources:

Directorate of History, Department of National Defence in
  Ottawa: Bishop's letters to his family.
University of Western Ontario: Bishop's combat reports.
War Amps of Canada: their digest *Hanging a Legend* was
  useful in my research.

Acknowledgements

I would like to acknowledge the help I received from a number of First World War veterans who crossed Bishop's path. These men, whom I interviewed or with whom I corresponded in the 1980s (plus one in 1993) include: George Stirrett, who served with the ace in the cavalry in 1915; Roger Neville, who was the pilot of Bishop's two-seater when the pair served at 21 Squadron in 1916; Harold Balfour, who taught Bishop how to fly; Tim Hervey, who took flight training with Bishop and later served with him at 60 Squadron; Willie Fry, who was Bishop's deputy flight leader in 1917; Tommy Williams, a First World War ace who knew Bishop personally; Otto Roosen, a former German pilot who claimed to have been shot down by Bishop; and Phil B. Townsend, a First World War pilot of 12 Squadron.

Index